WILLIAMS-SONOMA

Rustic Spanish

Hearty, authentic recipes for everyday cooking

PAUL RICHARDSON

photography
MAREN CARUSO

weldon**owen**

contents

When I first came to live in Spain, in 1989, I knew little about Spanish culinary culture beyond the classics of paella and gazpacho. In the years that followed, as I ate, talked, made friends, and observed local cooks in their kitchens, I came to realize this was a culinary universe with a depth and variety to rival those of Italy or France.

Since then, Spanish contemporary cuisine has taken the world by storm, with Ferran Adrià and the Roca brothers in the vanguard. With all due respect to those pioneering geniuses, however, it's Spanish country cooking that inspires me—especially since I've been living and working on my own organic farm in the rural hinterland of northern Extremadura. Here at home, what I cook and eat is rustic by necessity, since most of it proceeds from my own gardens, orchards, olive groves, henhouse, and pigsty.

Rural Spanish food is soulful, nourishing, and bursting with earthy, genuine flavors. Though often hearty, it is rarely indigestible or heavy. (And there's always the siesta, that great Spanish invention, to follow a ribsticking *cocido*, or a big rice with all the trimmings.) It is also as diverse as Spain's sixteen regions, its innumerable towns and villages, and its varied landscapes all the way from the chilly north to the tropical south. Like all cuisines worth bothering with, this one has its roots firmly in the land.

If I haven't taken too many liberties with the classic recipes in this book, it's partly because I haven't needed to. Centuries of limited resources and the realities of eating with the seasons have taught country cooks how to be ingenious and resourceful, how to make even humble foods interesting, and how to give a lift to an everyday staple with a transforming dose of punchy flavor.

Spanish cooking is wonderfully democratic. Some of its simplest dishes are masterpieces of folk art, and there are few recipes in this book that can't be followed successfully even by inexperienced cooks.

Rustic Spanish is informal food for family, friends, and communities, best prepared and enjoyed without too much fuss or ceremony. This is my kind of food. And soon, I hope, it'll be your kind of food too.

starters

In recent years tapas have taken off as a culinary genre in their own right, and the lazing, grazing Spanish lifestyle has caught the world's imagination. Plan your own tapas feast, kicking off with this quartet of aperitif-hour classics: sautéed almonds; marinated olives; piquant skewers called *gildas;* and fried padrón peppers.

mixed tapas

FOR THE SAUTÉED ALMONDS

1 cup (5½ oz/170 g) blanched whole Marcona almonds

2 tablespoons olive oil

2 teaspoons fresh thyme leaves

Fine sea salt

FOR THE MARINATED OLIVES

½ teaspoon cumin seeds

1 orange

2 cups (10 oz/315 g) mixed black and green olives

1 clove garlic, cut lengthwise into 4 slices

2 teaspoons chopped fresh flat-leaf parsley

½ teaspoon *pimentón dulce* (sweet Spanish smoked pepper)

¼ teaspoon red pepper flakes

¼ cup (60 ml) olive oil

To make the sautéed almonds, preheat the oven to 350°F (180°C). Spread the almonds in a single layer on a rimmed baking sheet and toast, stirring once or twice, until fragrant and just starting to color, about 8 minutes. Transfer immediately to a plate and let cool for 10 minutes.

In a frying pan, heat the olive oil over medium-high heat. Add the almonds and sauté, stirring constantly, until golden, 2–3 minutes. Using a slotted spoon, transfer the nuts to paper towels to drain.

Put the almonds in a serving bowl. Add the thyme and season to taste with salt. Using a fork, toss well. (Cover tightly and store at room temperature for up to 3 days.)

To make the marinated olives, in a small, dry frying pan, toast the cumin seeds over medium-high heat, stirring constantly, until fragrant, 2–3 minutes. Transfer to a saucepan.

Using a vegetable peeler, remove 3 strips of zest from the orange, each about 1 inch (2.5 cm) wide and 2 inches (5 cm) long. Cut each piece lengthwise into strips ¼ inch (6 mm) wide and add to the saucepan. Reserve the remaining zest and the orange for another use.

Add the olives, garlic, parsley, *pimentón,* red pepper flakes, and olive oil to the saucepan. Place over medium heat and toss to mix well. Heat until the oil starts to bubble around the edges of the pan. Reduce the heat to medium-low and cook, with the oil just bubbling occasionally, for 30 minutes, stirring now and then.

Transfer the contents of the saucepan to a serving bowl. Let cool to room temperature, then let stand for at least 1 hour or up to 24 hours to allow the flavors to develop before serving. (Store the olives in an airtight container in the refrigerator for up to 2 weeks.)

continued

FOR THE GILDAS

8 green Basque pickled peppers (see Cook's Note)

8 cured anchovy fillets

8–16 large green olives, pitted

Extra-virgin olive oil for drizzling

FOR THE FRIED PADRÓN PEPPERS

½ cup (125 ml) olive oil

1 lb (500 g) padrón peppers (see Cook's Note)

Flor de Sal or other flaky sea salt

serves 6

To make the *gildas,* bend a Basque pickled pepper at the middle and push it onto a toothpick or wooden skewer. Push the toothpick or skewer into one half of the anchovy fillet, then a green olive, followed by the other half of the anchovy to curl around the olive. Repeat the process until you have used up all the peppers, anchovies, and olives. Place on a serving platter and drizzle with olive oil.

To make the padrón peppers, in a wide frying pan, heat the olive oil over high heat. Add the peppers and turn them rapidly in the oil until they are blistered all over, 2 minutes. Remove with a slotted spoon and pile onto a serving platter. Sprinkle with 1 teaspoon flaky sea salt, and serve hot.

COOK'S NOTE: Basque pickled peppers are long, green, and pickled in vinegar. They can be found in Spanish groceries and specialty food shops. Padrón peppers are notorious for their unpredictable spiciness. It's said in Spain that one in every ten of these little green peppers is spicy, while the other nine are sweet and mild.

WINE SUGGESTION: A WELL-CHILLED, BONE-DRY, APPETIZING MANZANILLA SHERRY FROM SANLÚCAR DE BARRAMEDA

If ever there were to be a straw poll of Spain's most popular, as well as economical, dishes, *patatas bravas* would surely come in near the top. This super snack combines fried potato chunks with the piquant sauce that explains the epithet *"bravas"* ("fierce, wild"). Some versions add *allioli* (page 180) to the sauce for a smoother, richer consistency.

patatas bravas

Olive oil for frying

2 lb (1 kg) new potatoes, cut into 2-inch (5-cm) chunks if needed

1 heaping tablespoon flour

1 teaspoon *pimentón picante* (hot Spanish smoked pepper)

1 teaspoon *pimentón dulce* (sweet Spanish smoked pepper)

1 cup (8 fl oz/250 ml) beef stock, preferably homemade (page 179)

2 tablespoons red wine vinegar

½ cup (125 ml) tomato sauce

Fine sea salt

serves 8

Preheat the oven to 250°F (130°C). Pour olive oil into a large, deep frying pan to a depth of 1½ inches (4 cm) and heat over medium heat until hot. Add the potatoes and more oil if necessary to cover, reduce the heat to low, and cook until the potatoes are tender, 20–30 minutes. Raise the heat to high and allow them to brown. Using a slotted spoon, transfer the potatoes to an ovenproof terra-cotta casserole dish or baking dish and keep warm in the oven.

Pour off all but 1 tablespoon of the oil from the pan. Add the flour and both types of *pimentón* and stir over low heat for a few minutes. Slowly add the stock, stirring constantly. Then add the vinegar and simmer for about 10 minutes. Stir in the tomato sauce and a generous pinch of salt. Taste and adjust the seasoning.

Pour the sauce over the potatoes and serve warm.

PAIRING SUGGESTION: AN ICE-COLD SPANISH BEER

The eggplant is a versatile vegetable that happily lends itself to almost any cooking method, but roasting or grilling seems to bring out the best in it. This Catalan recipe usually involves barbecuing, but even oven-roasting gives the eggplant a delicious smoky flavor. *Escalivada* makes an ideal accompaniment for roast or grilled meats.

escalivada

2 yellow or red onions, unpeeled

Olive oil for rubbing the onions, plus 1 cup (250 ml) extra-virgin olive oil

3 eggplants

3 tomatoes

2 red bell peppers

½ cup (125 ml) fresh lemon juice

3 cloves garlic, minced

Fine sea salt and freshly ground black pepper

Chopped fresh flat-leaf parsley for garnish

serves 6–8

Preheat the oven to 400°F (200°C). Put the onions in a small baking pan and rub them with olive oil. Roast until tender when pierced, at least 1 hour. Let stand until cool enough to handle, then peel and slice ½ inch (12 mm) thick.

At the same time, prick the eggplants in several places with a fork and place them in their own baking pan. Add the tomatoes and place in the oven alongside the onions. Roast the tomatoes until their skins blacken, about 15 minutes. Let stand until cool enough to handle, then peel and cut into cubes. Continue to roast the eggplants until soft but not mushy, about 45 minutes more. Let cool, then peel and tear into large strips. Place in a colander to drain.

Position a rack 4–6 inches (10–15 cm) below the heat source and turn on the broiler. Cut the bell peppers in half lengthwise and remove the stems, seeds, and ribs. Place, cut sides down, on a baking sheet. Broil until the skins blacken and blister, about 10 minutes. Remove from the broiler, drape with aluminum foil, let cool for 10 minutes, then peel away the skins. Cut the peppers into long, narrow strips.

Combine the onions, eggplants, tomatoes, and peppers in a large bowl. In a small bowl, whisk together the olive oil, the lemon juice, and the garlic. Season with salt and pepper. Pour over the eggplant mixture and toss to coat well. Taste and adjust the seasoning. Sprinkle with parsley and serve.

WINE SUGGESTION: A FULL-BODIED CATALAN RED FROM THE PENEDÈS

This dish was all the rage in the late 1980s, when I first arrived in Spain. I assumed it had been around for ages, whereas in fact it had only been invented quite recently. Either way, it's now a classic, and with good reason—the piquant blue cheese and crunchy walnuts provide a perfect foil for the cool sweetness of Belgian endive.

endive with blue cheese dressing & walnuts

18–20 Belgian endive leaves

3½ oz (105 g) Cabrales, Roquefort, or other blue cheese

2 oz (60 g) cream cheese, at room temperature

¼ cup (60 ml) extra-virgin olive oil

Freshly ground black pepper

18–20 walnut halves, roughly chopped

serves 6

Arrange the endive leaves on a serving platter.

Crumble the blue cheese into a small bowl. Add the cream cheese and mash the cheeses together with a fork, then add the olive oil in a thin stream and continue blending them into a paste. Season with pepper.

Place a tablespoonful of the cheese mixture at the pointed end of each endive leaf. Sprinkle each with a few walnut pieces, and serve. (The endive leaves are best picked up at the stem end and eaten with the fingers.)

WINE SUGGESTION: A RICH, DRY OLOROSO OR AMONTILLADO SHERRY

Many years ago, in the tapas bar El Bocaito in Madrid, I ordered a dish described as *"perdices de mi huerta"*—"partridges from my garden." I expected a rich game stew, so imagine my surprise when I was served a plate of … lettuces! This simple starter relies on a genial combination of crisp, sweet lettuce hearts and the salty tang of anchovies.

lettuce hearts with cured anchovies

4 heads Little Gem lettuce or 4 romaine lettuce hearts (outer leaves removed)

1 tin (1¾ oz/50 g) cured anchovy fillets

Extra-virgin olive oil for drizzling

Freshly ground black pepper (optional)

serves 4–6

Wash and dry the lettuces, cutting away the hard stem at the base. Slice each one lengthwise into quarters.

Arrange the lettuce quarters side by side on a serving platter and lay an anchovy fillet along each one. Drizzle with plenty of olive oil and season with black pepper, if you like.

WINE SUGGESTION: AN ICE-COLD GLASS OF MANZANILLA SHERRY

The *calçotada* is a springtime celebration in which the season's first new spring onions *(calçots)* are roasted over coals until the outer skins are blackened and the interiors are sweet and toothsome. Originating in the town of Valls, near Tarragona, the custom has now spread as far as Barcelona. The point of the *calçotada* is the contrast between the partly caramelized, tender onions and the sensational, richly nutty sauce.

grilled spring onions with romesco sauce

FOR THE ROMESCO SAUCE

1 head garlic

2 ripe tomatoes

¾ cup (4 oz/125 g) blanched almonds, toasted

½ cup (2 oz/60 g) hazelnuts, toasted and skinned

4 small day-old baguette slices

½ cup (125 ml) extra-virgin olive oil, or as needed

2 tablespoons red wine vinegar, or as needed

1 teaspoon *pimentón dulce* (see Cook's Note)

Fine sea salt

24 true spring onions, each about 1 inch (2.5 cm) wide at the base and with plenty of white flesh

Crusty bread for serving

serves 4

To make the romesco, prepare a hot fire in a charcoal grill or preheat a gas grill on high. Grill the garlic, turning until browned on all sides, 13–15 minutes. Grill the tomatoes, turning once, until the skins are browned and wrinkled, about 5 minutes. Let the garlic and tomatoes cool, then peel.

Meanwhile, place the spring onions on the grill and cook, turning occasionally, until the outer skins have blackened and shriveled, about 8 minutes. Wrap the onions in newspaper and let stand until cool enough to handle, about 5 minutes.

Put the peeled garlic and tomatoes, nuts, and baguette slices in a food processor and pulse to combine. Mix in the olive oil, vinegar, *pimentón*, and salt to taste. The finished sauce should be thick but not dry; add more oil and vinegar if needed. Divide among individual dipping bowls and set aside. (The sauce will keep in an airtight container in the refrigerator for up to 5 days; bring to room temperature before serving.)

Transfer the onions to a large serving platter or a wooden board. Serve with crusty bread. Invite diners to peel the onions with their fingers and dip them into the romesco sauce.

COOK'S NOTE: Spanish *pimentón*, a spice made from dried smoked red peppers, is available as *dulce* (sweet), *agridulce* (bittersweet), and *picante* (spicy), *dulce* being the most commonly used. Paprika is no substitute.

WINE SUGGESTION: A SLIGHTLY CHILLED, YOUNG, LIGHT-BODIED RIOJA

Chef Javier Sánchez Bruno, a friend of mine born and raised in Tenerife, introduced to me this piquant mixture of cured goat cheese, tomato, and spicy peppers, a specialty of the Canary Islands. It lies somewhere between a sauce, a pâté, and a dip. I like to serve it with hot toast and, in summer, with crisp crudités.

almogrote

1 large ripe tomato, peeled, seeded, and roughly chopped

8 oz (250 g) cured goat cheese or other hard, strong cheese, cut into ¼-inch (6-mm) cubes

2 cloves garlic, minced

¼ cup (60 ml) extra-virgin olive oil, plus more for drizzling

1 tablespoon *pimentón dulce* (sweet Spanish smoked pepper)

1 teaspoon *pimentón picante* (hot Spanish smoked pepper) or cayenne pepper

FOR SERVING

Hot toast, crackers, or breadsticks; alternatively, batons of raw carrot, cucumber, radish, fennel, or other crisp raw vegetables

serves 4–6

Blitz the tomato, cheese, and garlic in a blender, then add the olive oil in a thin stream and blend for a few more seconds. The consistency should be neither runny nor excessively thick, and the color a creamy orange with specks of cheese still visible.

Transfer to a serving dish. Just before serving, make a small well in the *almogrote* and drizzle with olive oil and dust with both types of *pimentón*. Serve with toast or other crisp bread for topping or dipping, or surround with vegetables for diners to help themselves.

COOK'S NOTE: In the Canary Islands, dried red peppers are used, but *pimentón* makes a good alternative. I use a combination of sweet and spicy *pimentón* for this dish.

WINE SUGGESTION: A STRONG, AROMATIC WHITE FROM THE ISLAND OF TENERIFE

Escabeche is the Spanish technique of marinating poached or fried fish—or indeed rabbit or game—in an acidic mixture made with vinegar and aromatics. This light and fragrant tuna pickle is especially welcome on a hot day: serve it atop a mixed green salad and you've got yourself a perfect summer lunch.

tuna in escabeche

3 tablespoons olive oil

1½ lb (750 g) albacore or yellowfin tuna fillet, about 1 inch (2.5 cm) thick, cut into 6–8 pieces

1 red bell pepper, seeded and thinly sliced

½ red onion, thinly sliced

1 cup (250 ml) dry white wine

¾ cup (180 ml) sherry vinegar

2 cloves garlic, crushed

½ teaspoon whole black peppercorns

1 teaspoon finely grated orange zest

1 teaspoon sugar

Fine sea salt

½ teaspoon red pepper flakes

½ cup (2½ oz/75 g) pitted green olives such as Manzanilla

serves 4–6

In a large frying pan, heat 2 tablespoons of the olive oil over medium-high heat. When the oil is hot, add the tuna and cook, turning once, until browned on both sides but still pink in the center when tested with a knife, 5–8 minutes total. Transfer to a 2-qt (2-l) nonaluminum baking dish.

In the same pan, heat the remaining 1 tablespoon olive oil over medium-high heat. Add the bell pepper and onion and sauté until softened, 3–5 minutes. Add the wine, vinegar, garlic, peppercorns, orange zest, sugar, ¾ teaspoon salt, the red pepper flakes, and ¼ cup (60 ml) water and bring to a boil.

Pour the hot marinade and vegetables over the fish and scatter the olives over the top. Let cool to room temperature. Cover and refrigerate for at least 8 hours or up to 24 hours, turning the fish occasionally.

To serve, lift the tuna from the marinade and arrange on a serving platter. Pour off the marinade, reserving the vegetables and olives, and arrange them over the tuna. Let stand at room temperature for 15 minutes to bring out the flavors and then serve.

WINE SUGGESTION: A BONE-DRY FINO SHERRY

This classic Spanish tapa traditionally arrives at the table sizzling in a little metal pan. Sherry and lemon juice are not always used, but add a nice contrast to the richness of the olive oil and garlic.

sizzling garlic shrimp

4–5 tablespoons (60–75 ml) olive oil

4 cloves garlic, finely minced

1 teaspoon red pepper flakes

1 teaspoon *pimentón dulce* (sweet Spanish smoked pepper)

1 lb (500 g) medium shrimp, peeled and deveined if desired

1–2 tablespoons fresh lemon juice

1–2 tablespoons dry sherry

Fine sea salt and freshly ground black pepper

2 tablespoons chopped fresh flat-leaf parsley

Crusty bread for serving

serves 4

In a sauté pan, heat the olive oil over medium heat. Add the garlic, red pepper flakes, and *pimentón* and sauté until fragrant, about 1 minute. Raise the heat to high, add the shrimp, lemon juice, and sherry, and stir well. Sauté until the shrimp turn pink and are opaque throughout, about 3 minutes. Season with salt and pepper, sprinkle with the parsley, and serve with plenty of bread to sop up all the delicious pan juices.

WINE SUGGESTION: AN EASY-DRINKING WHITE FROM THE SOUTH OF SPAIN LIKE A PALOMINO FINA

Spanish piquillo peppers are traditionally handpicked, then roasted in wood-fired ovens before being peeled and packed, the woodsmoke enhancing their distinctively sweet, slightly spicy flavor. These small, triangular peppers lend themselves to stuffing with a variety of fillings, from meat and rice to the creamy salt cod purée called *brandada*.

piquillo peppers stuffed with salt cod brandada

FOR THE BRANDADA

2 medium all-purpose potatoes

1¼ lb (20 oz/625 g) desalted salt cod (see Cook's Note)

1 cup (250 ml) olive oil

4 cloves garlic

½ cup (125 ml) half-and-half

Fine sea salt if needed and freshly ground black pepper

1 jar (12 oz/375 g) roasted piquillo peppers (about 12 peppers)

1 tablespoon extra-virgin olive oil

Position a rack 4–6 inches (10–15 cm) below the heat source and turn on the broiler.

To make the *brandada*, put the potatoes in a pot and add water to cover by 2 inches (5 cm). Bring to a boil, then reduce the heat to medium-high and cook until tender, about 15 minutes. Drain and roughly chop.

Pat the desalted cod dry with paper towels. In a small, heavy sauté pan, heat the olive oil over low heat and gently sauté the garlic until golden brown, 1–2 minutes. Remove and discard the garlic, reserving the oil. Take the pan off the heat and let cool a little. Off the heat, carefully place the cod fillets in the hot oil and poach, turning once, about 5 minutes. Using a slotted spoon, transfer to a blender or food processor, reserving the oil.

Add the potatoes and the half-and-half to the blender and season with pepper. Blend the mixture into a thick cream. Taste for salt (you will probably not have to add any) and add 3 tablespoons of the garlic oil used to poach the cod. The *brandada* should not be too liquid—hold back on the oil if need be. Set aside.

Drain the peppers, but do not rinse. With your fingers, gently open the stem end of each pepper.

With a small spoon or your fingers, carefully stuff about 1 tablespoon of the *brandada* inside each pepper. The *brandada* should fill the peppers but should not be bursting out.

Position a rack 4–6 inches (10–15 cm) below the heat source and turn on the broiler. Arrange the peppers in a single layer on a rimmed baking sheet. Brush them with the olive oil. Broil until the filling is bubbling, about 7 minutes. Let cool slightly.

FOR THE VINAIGRETTE

⅓ cup (80 ml) extra-virgin olive oil

3½ tablespoons balsamic vinegar

1 small shallot, minced

Flaky sea salt and freshly ground black pepper

Finely chopped fresh chives for garnish

serves 4

Meanwhile, make the vinaigrette. In a small bowl, whisk together the olive oil, vinegar, shallot, ½ teaspoon flaky salt, and ¼ teaspoon pepper.

Transfer the peppers to a serving platter. Drizzle liberally with the vinaigrette, sprinkle with chives, and serve at once.

COOK'S NOTE: If using frozen desalted cod, thaw and drain thoroughly. If using salt cod, desalt the fish by soaking it in cold water in the refrigerator for 2 days, changing the water twice a day. Drain thoroughly in a colander.

WINE SUGGESTION: AN ELEGANT, WELL-STRUCTURED, OAKED RIOJA CRIANZA

With all due respect to the French *moules marinières*, this is the best way I know to make the most of mussels. Refreshing and light, with a tang of vinegar and lime, it's the perfect starter for a lazy lunch on a hot summer day.

cold mussels salpicón

4 lb (2 kg) live mussels

Juice of 1 lime

1 red bell pepper, seeded and finely chopped

1 green bell pepper, seeded and finely chopped

1 small red onion, finely chopped

½ cup (125 ml) extra-virgin olive oil

¼ cup (60 ml) white wine vinegar

4 sprigs fresh flat-leaf parsley, leaves minced

Fine sea salt

serves 4

Scrub and rinse the mussels under cold water, debearding if necessary. Discard any that do not close to the touch.

In a saucepan, combine 1 cup (250 ml) water and the lime juice and bring to a boil. Add the mussels, cover, and reduce the heat to medium. Cook until the mussels have opened, shaking the pan from time to time and stirring once. Discard any that fail to open.

Drain, reserving the stock. Allow the mussels to cool, then open with your hands, reserving the shell half with the mussel flesh and discarding the other half. Arrange the mussels on a serving platter. Place in the fridge.

Meanwhile, make the salpicón. Combine the peppers and onion in a glass bowl and add the olive oil, vinegar, parsley, and salt to taste. Add ¼ cup (60 ml) of the reserved mussel stock and mix well.

Spoon this mixture over the mussels and return them to the fridge to chill well. Serve chilled.

WINE SUGGESTION: AN APPLEY, FRESH WHITE TXAKOLI FROM THE BASQUE COUNTRY

These golden fritters—called *tortillitas*, as they resemble little omelets—are one of the joys of a visit to Cádiz. This is a city that knows how to fry, and Cádiz's best *tortillitas* manage to be wafer-thin, deliciously crisp, and never greasy. These fritters contain no egg, making them reminiscent of Japanese tempura.

cádiz-style shrimp fritters

2 cups (10 oz/315 g) bread flour

2 cups (500 ml) ice-cold water

Fine sea salt

5 oz (155 g) bay shrimp

1 yellow onion, finely chopped

½ cup (¾ oz/20 g) fresh flat-leaf parsley leaves, roughly chopped

Oil for frying (olive oil or a mixture of olive and sunflower oils)

serves 4–6 (makes about 20 fritters)

Put the flour in a large bowl and whisk in the water little by little to prevent lumps from forming. The batter should be smooth and creamy in consistency, but not too thick. Add 1 tablespoon salt, then fold in the shrimp, onion, and parsley. Cover and place in the fridge for at least 15 minutes.

Pour the oil to a finger's depth in a frying pan and heat over medium-high heat until the oil is smoking hot. Using a small metal ladle, add a spoonful of batter to the hot oil, spreading it a little to ensure thinness. Fry 2 fritters at a time: do not crowd the pan.

Using a flat, holed implement or skimmer (the Spanish *espumadera* is ideal), baste the fritters a little with the oil, removing any stray drops of batter that may otherwise burn. When golden on the first side, turn over with the help of a fork and brown on the second side. Transfer to paper towels to drain. Serve piping hot.

COOK'S NOTE: A little practice may be needed to achieve the proper thinness for the *tortillitas*. Don't be afraid to spread out the batter in the hot oil—the batter is surprisingly resilient.

WINE SUGGESTION: A LIP-SMACKINGLY FRESH FINO SHERRY OR MANZANILLA DE SANLÚCAR

This dish has its roots in the economical cooking of a less prosperous time in Europe, when meat was a valuable commodity and to throw away food leftovers was unthinkable. The remains of the Sunday lunch would find their way into *croquetas* on Monday. Nowadays, they make a tasty snack.

croquettes with chicken & ham

3 tablespoons olive oil, plus more for frying

3 tablespoons flour

1½ cups (350 ml) whole milk

1½ cups (12 fl oz/350 ml) chicken stock, preferably homemade (page 178)

⅓ cup (2 oz/60 g) finely chopped cooked chicken

⅓ cup (2 oz/60 g) finely chopped serrano ham

Pinch of freshly grated nutmeg

Fine sea salt and freshly ground black pepper

1 cup (4 oz/125 g) fine dried bread crumbs

2 large eggs

serves 4–6

In a small, heavy saucepan over low heat, combine the olive oil and the flour. Cook, stirring constantly, until the flour has absorbed all of the oil, 2–3 minutes. Add the milk and stock, little by little, stirring constantly with a wooden spoon. (Use a whisk to smooth out the mixture if lumps start to form.) Cook the sauce, continuing to stir constantly, until smooth and thick, 10–15 minutes. Remove from the heat, stir in the chicken, ham, and nutmeg, and season to taste with salt and pepper.

Pour the mixture into a metal baking pan and let cool to room temperature. Cover with plastic wrap and refrigerate overnight. By the next day, the mixture will have congealed into a thick paste.

Put the bread crumbs in a shallow bowl. In a second shallow bowl, lightly beat the eggs. Using a spoon and your hands, form the chilled paste into logs 2 inches (5 cm) long and about 1 inch (2.5 cm) in diameter. Roll them once in the bread crumbs, then in the beaten eggs, and then again in the bread crumbs, making sure each croquette is thoroughly coated.

Pour olive oil into a large frying pan to a depth of 1 inch (2.5 cm) and heat over medium-high heat until very hot. Slip in the croquettes a few at a time and fry, turning once, until golden brown, about 3 minutes in all. Transfer to paper towels to drain. Serve at once.

WINE SUGGESTION: A ROBUST AND PLUMMY CABERNET SAUVIGNON FROM MADRID

These flavorful pork skewers are part of the intriguing Moorish culinary legacy in Spain. Of course, the Moors were Muslim and did not eat pork, but Christian Spaniards borrowed the delicious North African spice combination traditionally used on lamb kebabs and applied it to their beloved meat.

moorish-spiced pork kebabs

½ cup (125 ml) olive oil

3 tablespoons ground cumin

2 tablespoons ground coriander

1 tablespoon *pimentón dulce* (sweet Spanish smoked pepper)

1½ teaspoons cayenne pepper

1 teaspoon ground turmeric

1 teaspoon dried oregano

Fine sea salt and freshly ground black pepper

2 lb (1 kg) pork loin, cut into 1-inch (2.5-cm) cubes

2 tablespoons minced garlic

¼ cup (⅓ oz/10 g) chopped fresh flat-leaf parsley

¼ cup (60 ml) fresh lemon juice

Lemon wedges for serving

serves 8

In a small frying pan, combine the olive oil, cumin, coriander, *pimentón*, cayenne, turmeric, oregano, 1 teaspoon salt, and ½ teaspoon black pepper. Place over low heat until warmed through and fragrant, about 3 minutes. Remove from the heat and let cool to room temperature.

Place the pork pieces in a bowl and rub with the spice mixture. Add the garlic, parsley, and lemon juice and toss well. Cover and refrigerate overnight.

The next day, position a rack 4–6 inches (10–15 cm) below the heat source and turn on the broiler, or prepare a hot fire in a charcoal grill or preheat a gas grill on high. Thread the meat onto skewers and sprinkle with salt.

Place on a broiler pan or the grill rack and broil or grill, turning once, until just cooked through, about 4 minutes on each side. Transfer to a platter and serve with lemon wedges.

WINE SUGGESTION: A RIPE ANDALUCÍAN RED LIKE FINCA MONCLOA

Traditionally, this pâté is wrapped in pig's caul, the lacelike fat that surrounds the pig's stomach, and baked. A bacon wrapping will work just as well. It's an easy-to-make rustic Catalan dish, influenced by the cooking of neighboring southwest France. Serve with greens, toasted walnuts, pickles, and hot toast.

country-style pâté of pork liver

2 slices coarse country white bread (about 2 oz/60 g), crusts removed

½ cup (125 ml) whole milk

7 oz (220 g) pork liver, trimmed and minced

10 oz (315 g) pork loin, minced

14 oz (400 g) pancetta or unsmoked bacon, minced

3 large eggs, beaten

1 tablespoon good-quality brandy

Generous handful fresh flat-leaf parsley leaves, minced

4 cloves garlic, minced

1 teaspoon *each pimentón dulce* (sweet Spanish smoked pepper), ground cinnamon, ground coriander, and fresh thyme leaves

Fine sea salt and freshly ground black pepper

16 thin slices bacon or 1 pig's caul

Boiling water as needed

serves 8

Preheat the oven to 425°F (220°C). In a bowl, soak the bread in the milk for 2 minutes. Squeeze out the milk, then mince the bread.

In a large bowl, combine the pork liver, pork loin, and pancetta. Add the eggs, minced bread, brandy, parsley, garlic, *pimentón,* cinnamon, coriander, thyme, 1 heaping teaspoon salt, and a little pepper. Mix everything together thoroughly into a pâté.

Line a 1-qt (1-l) terrine with the bacon slices, laying them across the mold and letting the ends hang over the sides, or line the terrine with the caul. Spoon in the pâté mixture, pressing down gently to prevent air bubbles from forming. Fold the bacon or caul over, enclosing the pâté.

Place the terrine in a baking pan and add boiling water to reach halfway up the sides of the mold. Bake, uncovered, until the top begins to brown, about 45 minutes. Cover and continue to bake until cooked through, about 45 minutes longer. Let cool completely.

To make the pâté compact and easily sliceable, cut a piece of cardboard to fit inside the terrine and wrap it with aluminum foil. Place it on the surface of the pâté and place a heavy weight on top. Transfer to the refrigerator to chill for at least 12 hours or up to 24 hours.

To serve, remove the weight and cardboard and turn the pâté out onto a serving platter. If the pâté won't come out of the terrine, warm the base in a bowl of hot water, and try again. Slice and serve.

WINE SUGGESTION: AN ELEGANT SPANISH CHARDONNAY

How something so simple and apparently artless could have come to such prominence is one of the mysteries of Spanish food. Tomato bread is particularly good in summer, when tomatoes are ripe, sweet, and full of flavor, and in winter, when fresh olive oil is running off the presses and still has a fruity taste and golden color.

pa amb tomàquet

1 ciabatta or 8 slices coarse country white bread, preferably sourdough

4 cloves garlic, halved (optional)

4 small ripe tomatoes

Extra-virgin olive oil for drizzling

Flaky sea salt

OPTIONAL TOPPINGS

Thin slices serrano ham or other cured meat

Olive oil–packed anchovy fillets or other marinated fish

Thin slices sheep's milk cheese such as *Idiazábal*

Escalivada (page 17)

Grilled fresh pork sausages or baby lamb chops

serves 4

Prepare a hot fire in a charcoal grill or preheat a gas grill to high. Alternatively, position a rack 4–6 inches (10–15 cm) below the heat source and turn on the broiler. If using ciabatta, slice it crosswise into 4–6 pieces, then cut each piece in half horizontally. Place the bread on the grill rack or on a baking sheet. Grill or broil, turning once, until golden brown on both sides, about 2 minutes on each side.

While the toasts are still warm, rub them on one side with the cut sides of the garlic halves, if using. Cut each tomato in half crosswise. Rub the cut sides of the tomato halves over the toasts until only the skins are left, then discard the skins. Drizzle with olive oil and sprinkle with flaky salt to taste. If using sliced sourdough, cut the toasts in half. Pile the toasts on a serving platter or in a shallow bowl and serve with optional toppings, if desired.

WINE SUGGESTION: A YOUNG, FLAVOR-PACKED, LIGHTLY CHILLED RED WINE FROM THE PENEDÈS

The *bocadillo* is the Spanish sandwich, a hunk of bread stuffed with cheese, ham, *salchichón* or chorizo sausage, deep-fried squid rings, or whatever else takes your fancy. *Bocadillos* are eaten any time of the day, but especially in late morning, in the late afternoon, and late at night after a hard evening of fiesta.

bocadillos with cheese, anchovies & peppers

2 large red bell peppers

2 baguettes, cut into 6-inch (15-cm) lengths

4 small ripe tomatoes

Extra-virgin olive oil for drizzling

Fine sea salt

4 thin slices fresh cheese, such as *queso fresco de Burgos*

8 olive oil–packed anchovy fillets

makes 4 sandwiches

Preheat the oven to 450°F (230°C). Place the bell peppers on a baking sheet and roast, turning several times to cook evenly, until the skins are blistered and blackened all over, about 45 minutes. Transfer the peppers to a paper bag, close the bag, and let the peppers steam until cool enough to handle, about 15 minutes. Peel off the charred skins. Slice each bell pepper in half lengthwise and discard the stems, seeds, and ribs. Cut the peppers into strips and set aside. (The roasted peppers will keep for up to a week in the refrigerator with a covering of olive oil.)

Position a rack 4–6 inches (10–15 cm) below the heat source and turn on the broiler. Cut each length of baguette in half horizontally. Transfer the baguette halves, cut side up, to a baking sheet and broil until lightly toasted, about 1 minute.

Cut each tomato in half crosswise. Rub the cut sides of the tomato halves on the toasted baguette surfaces until only the skins are left, then discard the skins. Drizzle with olive oil and sprinkle with salt to taste.

Divide the cheese slices evenly among the bottom halves of the baguettes, followed by the roasted bell pepper strips and anchovies. Cover with the top halves of the baguette and press gently to secure the filling. Cut each sandwich in half again, if desired, and serve at once.

PAIRING SUGGESTION: AN ICE-COLD CAN OF COKE, SPRITE, OR SAN MIGUEL BEER

One of the culinary delights of Spain's Catalan-speaking regions are *coques*, a thin-crusted Spanish take on pizza. Their toppings might include eggplant and peppers, onions and raisins, spinach and pine nuts, or cured anchovies. No self-respecting bakery in Catalunya is without a tasty *coca* on the counter.

catalan-style flatbreads

1 risen ball flatbread dough (page 180)

1 red bell pepper

1 green bell pepper

1 eggplant

1 clove garlic, crushed

12 black olives, pitted and coarsely chopped

Fine sea salt and freshly ground black pepper

2 large, ripe tomatoes, thinly sliced

4 tablespoons (60 ml) olive oil

serves 6

COCA WITH PEPPER, EGGPLANT & OLIVE TOPPING

Preheat the oven to 450°F (230°C). Place the bell peppers and eggplant on a rimmed baking sheet and roast, turning several times to cook evenly, until the peppers are blistered and blackened all over and the skin of the eggplant is wrinkled and shriveled, about 45 minutes. Transfer the peppers and eggplant to a paper bag, close the bag, and let steam until cool enough to handle, about 15 minutes. Peel off the charred skins and remove the stems and bell pepper seeds and ribs. Cut the peppers and eggplant into strips. Leave the oven on, reducing the heat to 350°F (180°C).

In a large bowl, combine the bell pepper and eggplant strips with the garlic and olives and season generously with salt and pepper.

Lightly oil a 9-by-12-inch (23-by-30-cm) rimmed baking sheet. On a lightly floured work surface, roll out the dough into a rectangle to fit the pan. Press into the prepared pan and trim away any excess dough.

Cover the dough with the tomato slices and drizzle with 2 tablespoons of the olive oil. Arrange the pepper and eggplant mixture evenly over the tomatoes and drizzle with the remaining 2 tablespoons olive oil.

Bake the *coca* until the edges are beginning to brown, about 40 minutes. Let cool slightly, then cut into squares and serve warm.

1 risen ball flatbread dough
(page 180)

2½ lb (1.25 kg) spinach

½ cup (125 ml) olive oil,
plus 2 tablespoons

4 cloves garlic, thinly sliced

Fine sea salt and freshly
ground black pepper

6 tablespoons (2 oz/60 g)
pine nuts

⅓ cup (2 oz/60 g) raisins

serves 6

COCA WITH SPINACH, PINE NUT & RAISIN TOPPING

Preheat the oven to 350°F (180°C). Wash the spinach leaves well, trim
off the thick stems, roughly chop the leaves, and dry them thoroughly
in a salad spinner.

In a large, deep frying pan, heat the ½ cup (125 ml) olive oil over medium
heat. Add the garlic slices and sauté until just beginning to color,
1–2 minutes. Add the spinach and 1 teaspoon salt, then turn the spinach
over in the oil until it has darkened and reduced in volume, about
4 minutes. Stir in the pine nuts and raisins and season well with pepper.

Lightly oil a 9-by-12-inch (23-by-30-cm) rimmed baking sheet. On a lightly
floured work surface, roll out the dough into a rectangle to fit the pan.
Press into the prepared pan and trim away any excess dough.

Spread the spinach mixture evenly over the dough and drizzle with
the 2 tablespoons olive oil. Bake the *coca* until the edges are beginning
to brown, about 40 minutes. Let cool slightly, then cut into squares
and serve warm.

WINE SUGGESTION: A SMOOTH, FRUITY RIOJA

soups & salads

The association between hard squash and the season of fall is a close one, and this soup is made even more autumnal with a haunting hint of smoky *pimentón de la Vera*—the Spanish spice made by grinding dried, smoked red peppers. Though luxuriously rich and creamy, this recipe contains no dairy products.

butternut soup with pimentón

2 lb (1 kg) butternut squash

2 tablespoons olive oil

1 red onion, coarsely chopped

1 rib celery, chopped

1 carrot, chopped

2 cloves garlic, peeled and crushed

1 bay leaf

1 sprig fresh rosemary

4 fresh sage leaves

½ tablespoon *pimentón* (Spanish smoked pepper)

1 qt (32 fl oz/1 l) chicken stock, preferably homemade (page 178)

Fine sea salt and freshly ground black pepper

FOR THE CROUTONS

1 tablespoon olive oil

4 oz (125 g) semicured chorizo sausage, peeled and chopped

3 thick slices brown bread (about 6 oz/170 g), crusts removed and bread cut into 1-inch (2.5-cm) dice

1 small bunch fresh chives

serves 4

Halve, seed, and skin the butternut squash, then cut the flesh into 4-inch (10-cm) chunks. Set aside.

In a heavy saucepan, heat the olive oil over medium heat. Add the onion, celery, carrot, garlic, bay leaf, rosemary, and sage and gently sauté until the onions are soft and fragrant, 8–10 minutes. Stir in the *pimentón*.

Add the butternut squash and stock, season well with salt and pepper, cover, and simmer until the squash is soft, about 30 minutes. Let cool a little.

Remove and discard the bay leaf and rosemary sprig. Ladle the soup into a food processor or blender and purée until velvety smooth. Taste and adjust the seasoning.

To make the croutons, in a small frying pan, heat the olive oil over medium heat. Add the chorizo and fry until it has released some of its fat. Add the bread and toss in the pan to absorb the chorizo juices, then sauté until the bread is browned and the chorizo crisp and dry. Tip the croutons into a bowl.

Finely snip the chives onto a small plate.

Ladle the soup into bowls and pass the croutons and chives around the table for diners to serve themselves.

WINE SUGGESTION: A FULL-BODIED, FRUITY CHARDONNAY FROM NAVARRA

Hailing from Murcia, *olla gitana* ("gypsy pot") is wonderfully rib-sticking and protein-rich, but surprisingly contains no meat. The pears, cumin seeds, and mint may seem like modern inclusions, but in fact are traditional and authentic. I've found this to be an ideal dish for feeding a party of hungry vegetarians.

winter squash, potato, pear & chickpea stew

1 lb (500 g) dried chickpeas, soaked in water overnight

1 bay leaf

1 lb (500 g) potatoes, peeled and coarsely chopped

12 oz (375 g) butternut squash or pumpkin, peeled, seeded, and coarsely chopped

3–4 ripe pears, peeled if desired, cored, and coarsely chopped

12 oz (375 g) romano beans or other green beans, cut into 2-inch (5-cm) pieces

FOR THE SOFRITO

3 tablespoons olive oil

1 yellow onion, finely chopped

2 cloves garlic, minced

1 tomato, peeled and finely chopped or grated

1 teaspoon cumin seed, ground in a mortar and pestle

Fine sea salt

1 teaspoon *pimentón* (Spanish smoked pepper)

1 handful fresh mint leaves

serves 6–8

Drain the chickpeas. In a heavy flameproof casserole dish or a stockpot, combine the chickpeas, 3 qt (3 l) cold water, and the bay leaf and bring to a boil. Reduce the heat to medium-low and simmer until the chickpeas are almost tender, about 45 minutes (see Cook's Note).

Add the potatoes and butternut squash and cook for 15 minutes longer.

Add the pears and green beans and cook until both are tender, 4–6 minutes.

Meanwhile, make the *sofrito*. In a frying pan, heat the olive oil over medium heat. Add the onion and sauté until just beginning to color, about 3 minutes, then add the garlic and sauté just until fragrant. Add the tomato, cumin, 1 teaspoon salt, and the *pimentón*. Mix well, reduce the heat to medium-low, and cook for a few more minutes. Add the *sofrito* to the chickpea stew.

Simmer gently, stirring occasionally, until the flavors have mingled and the chickpeas are completely soft.

Remove from the heat, cover, and let rest for 10 minutes. Stir in the mint leaves and serve.

Like other Spanish stews, *olla gitana* tastes even better the following day.

COOK'S NOTE: Cooking times for dried legumes can vary widely depending on whether the water used is hard or soft. These chickpeas, for example, cook much more quickly in soft water.

WINE SUGGESTION: A BIG, ROBUST MEDITERRANEAN RED FROM YECLA, MURCIA'S PREMIUM WINE REGION

This creamy soup, *ajoblanco*, is a staple in southern Spain. Finely ground almonds give it body, while grapes impart a refreshing contrast to the soup's vinegary tang. For a different effect, try replacing the grapes with balled ripe melon (a green-fleshed type such as Galia or honeydew is best) and a handful of chopped mint.

white gazpacho with grapes

1 piece baguette, about 6 inches (15 cm) long

1½ cups (6 oz/170 g) blanched flaked almonds, plus 2 tablespoons for garnish

2 cloves garlic, quartered

⅓ cup (80 ml) extra-virgin olive oil

3 cups (750 ml) ice water, or as needed

¼ cup (60 ml) white wine

2 teaspoons white wine vinegar

1 teaspoon sherry vinegar

Fine sea salt and freshly ground black pepper

1 cup (6 oz/170 g) seedless green grapes, peeled and halved

serves 4

In a large bowl, soak the bread in cold water until soft, about 1 minute, then drain. Tear into several chunks and squeeze out as much of the water as possible. Set aside.

In a blender or food processor, combine the 1½ cups (6 oz/170 g) almonds, the garlic, olive oil, and 1 cup (250 ml) of the ice water. Blitz until the nuts are very finely ground, about 2 minutes, stopping to scrape down the sides of the workbowl as needed.

Add the bread. With the motor running, pour in the remaining 2 cups (500 ml) ice water in a slow, steady stream. Process until the soup has the consistency of light cream, again stopping to scrape down the sides of the workbowl as needed. Add the wine and vinegars and process just to mix. Season to taste with salt and pepper. Pour the soup into an airtight container and refrigerate for at least 2 hours or up to overnight.

In a small, dry frying pan, toast the 2 tablespoons almonds over medium heat, stirring constantly, until golden, about 4 minutes. Transfer immediately to a plate and let cool.

The chilled soup will be as thick as stirred yogurt. Just before serving, if desired, thin it with ice water back to the consistency of cream. Adjust the seasoning with salt and pepper. Stir in the grapes. Ladle into bowls, garnish with the almonds and a few grindings of pepper, and serve.

WINE SUGGESTION: A RIPE, FULL-BODIED SPANISH CHARDONNAY FROM D.O. SOMANTANO

You'd be forgiven for thinking gazpacho the only cold Spanish soup. In fact, the genre is much wider, and gazpacho is only the best known. *Salmorejo,* from the city of Córdoba, is a first cousin of gazpacho yet tastes completely different, with a garlicky piquancy, velvety texture, and rich flavor resulting from lots of olive oil.

cold tomato & garlic soup

2 lb (1 kg) large, ripe tomatoes

4 thick slices good-quality country white bread (about 8 oz/250 g), crusts removed and bread coarsely chopped

1 clove garlic, peeled

Fine sea salt

1 cup (250 ml) extra-virgin olive oil, preferably Spanish

2 hard-boiled large eggs, peeled and finely chopped

4 oz (125 g) serrano ham, finely chopped

serves 6

With a small sharp knife, core each tomato. Put the tomatoes in a blender and blend to a thick purée. Strain through a sieve to remove the seeds and shreds of skin, then return to the blender. Stir in the bread and let steep for 10 minutes.

Add the garlic clove and 1 teaspoon salt and purée until the mixture is smooth. With the machine running, add the olive oil in a thin stream to achieve a glossy, thick soup. Pour the soup into an airtight container and refrigerate for at least 1 hour.

Serve in shallow soup bowls, sprinkling a little chopped hard-boiled egg and chopped ham in the center of each.

WINE SUGGESTION: A COLD GLASS OF FINO MONTILLA-MORILES, A SHERRY-LIKE WINE FROM CÓRDOBA PROVINCE

Gazpacho has come a long way since it was enjoyed by harvesters on the scorching plains of southern Spain. Modern versions now include all manner of novel ingredients, from carrots and ginger to beets, watermelon, and strawberries. This one, featuring cherries, is a contemporary classic and a personal favorite of mine.

cherry gazpacho

2½ lb (1.25 kg) ripe tomatoes

½ cup (2 oz/60 g) coarsely chopped white onion or green onions

1 clove garlic

3 tablespoons coarsely chopped green bell pepper

3 thick slices country-style white bread (about 6 oz/ 170 g), crusts removed and bread torn up

Fine sea salt

½ cup (120 ml) extra-virgin olive oil, or as needed

8 oz (250 g) cherries, pitted

¼ cup (60 ml) sherry vinegar, or as needed

FOR SERVING

Diced fresh cheese, halved pitted cherries, torn fresh basil leaves, and/or extra-virgin olive oil

serves 6

Peel the tomatoes (this may not be necessary if you have a powerful kitchen blender). Core the tomatoes and coarsely chop. Put the chopped tomatoes in a blender along with the onion, garlic, bell pepper, bread, salt to taste, and ¼ cup (60 ml) of the olive oil. Blitz to a smooth cream.

Add the cherries, the remaining ¼ cup (60 ml) olive oil, and the vinegar and blend until thoroughly combined. Add cold water as needed to reach the consistency of a thin soup, then give everything one final whizz. Taste and adjust the seasoning, adding a little more salt and/or vinegar if you like. Cover and chill for at least 1 hour.

Serve in soup plates or bowls and garnish with diced fresh cheese, halved cherries, torn basil leaves, and/or a few drops of good olive oil.

WINE SUGGESTION: A CHILLED GLASS OF FINO MONTILLA-MORILES, A SHERRY-LIKE WINE FROM ANDALUCÍA

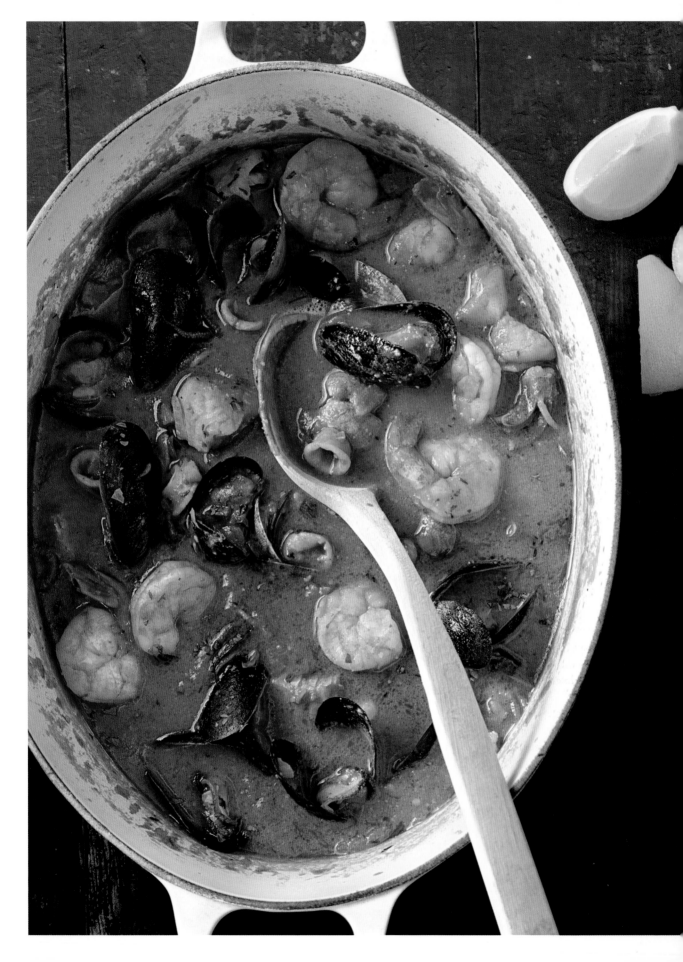

This Catalan fish stew, *zarzuela*, with its flavorful combination of fish and shellfish, is named after a centuries-old form of Spanish musical theater known for its colorful mix of characters. Serve the *zarzuela* with warm, crusty bread and quartered lemons for squeezing into the broth.

fish stew with saffron

3 lb (1.5 kg) mixed seafood such as live mussels and clams, striped bass, halibut, cleaned squid, and peeled and deveined shrimp

¼ teaspoon saffron threads

⅓ cup (1½ oz/45 g) blanched slivered almonds

2 tablespoons fresh flat-leaf parsley leaves

1 tablespoon lemon juice

1 clove garlic, coarsely chopped

1½ teaspoons *pimentón* (Spanish smoked pepper)

¼ cup (60 ml) olive oil

1 red bell pepper

1 green bell pepper

1 yellow onion, chopped

½ cup (125 ml) white wine

2 cups (16 fl oz/500 ml) fish stock, preferably homemade (page 178)

1 can (28 oz/875 g) crushed tomatoes

½ teaspoon dried thyme

½ cup (2½ oz/75 g) pitted green olives such as Manzanilla, chopped

Fine sea salt and freshly ground black pepper

serves 4–6

Scrub the mussels and clams well, if using. Debeard the mussels, if necessary. Put the shellfish in a bowl of water and refrigerate. Cut the fish into 1½-inch (4-cm) chunks. If using squid, cut the bodies into ½-inch (12-mm) rings. Put the seafood in a bowl and refrigerate.

In a small, dry frying pan, toast the saffron threads over medium heat, stirring constantly or shaking the pan, until fragrant and a shade darker, about 1 minute. Pour the threads into a bowl and, when cool, crumble with your fingertips. Set aside.

In a blender or food processor, combine the almonds, parsley, lemon juice, garlic, *pimentón,* and 2 tablespoons of the olive oil and whizz to a smooth purée. Set aside.

Remove the seeds, stems, and ribs from the bell peppers and chop the peppers. In a large Dutch oven, heat the remaining 2 tablespoons olive oil over medium heat. Add the onion and the peppers and sauté until softened, 8–10 minutes. Add the wine and cook until most of the liquid has evaporated, about 2 minutes. Stir in the stock, tomatoes, thyme, olives, saffron, and almond mixture and season generously with salt and pepper. Adjust the heat to maintain a simmer, cover, and cook for about 10 minutes to allow the flavors to blend.

Drain the mussels and clams and add to the pot, discarding any that do not close to the touch. Add the fish, cover, and simmer for about 5 minutes. Add the squid and shrimp, cover, and cook until the mussels and clams have opened and the fish and seafood are opaque throughout, about 5 minutes longer. Discard any mussels or clams that fail to open.

Ladle the stew into soup bowls and serve.

WINE SUGGESTION: A MEDITERRANEAN-STYLE WHITE FROM CATALUNYA LIKE TORRE'S GRAN VIÑA SOL

Karlos Arguiñano is Spain's most popular TV chef. A genial Basque with his own fine restaurant in the coastal town of Zarautz, Arguiñano has a gift for sharing the values of good old-fashioned Spanish home cooking. I first encountered his simple, hearty leek stew in the 1990s and have been making it regularly ever since.

basque leek & potato stew

¼ cup (60 ml) olive oil

1 yellow onion, finely chopped

6 leeks, white and pale green parts, trimmed and chopped

3 medium potatoes, chopped

2 carrots, chopped

2 qt (64 fl oz/2 l) chicken or vegetable stock, preferably homemade (page 178), heated

Fine sea salt and freshly ground black pepper

serves 4–6

In a flameproof casserole with a lid or Dutch oven over low heat, heat the olive oil and gently sauté the onion until tender, about 5 minutes (do not allow it to color).

Add the leeks, potatoes, and carrots, then pour in the hot stock. Season with salt and pepper, cover, and simmer until the vegetables are soft, about 20 minutes.

Serve the stew in soup plates.

WINE SUGGESTION: A SOFT, FRUITY PARELLADA-CHARDONNAY BLEND FROM THE PENEDÈS

This dish from my adopted home region of Extremadura can trace its origins back to the village of Jarandilla in the county of La Vera. It was near here, at Charles V's palace at Yuste, that the vegetable pepper made its entry into the Old World. And guess what? There are both peppers and *pimentón* in this down-home potato soup.

potato soup with eggs & peppers

½ cup (125 ml) olive oil

2 large potatoes, cut into ⅜-inch (1-cm) slices

1 teaspoon *pimentón* (Spanish smoked pepper)

Hot water as needed

2 green bell peppers, seeded and thinly sliced

1 red bell pepper, seeded and thinly sliced

1 bay leaf

Fine sea salt

1 clove garlic, minced

2 large eggs, beaten

4 thick slices country bread (about 8 oz/250 g)

serves 4

In a flameproof shallow terra-cotta or cast-iron casserole dish or in a Dutch oven, heat the olive oil over medium heat. When the oil is hot, add the potatoes and sauté until almost soft, about 5 minutes.

Sprinkle the *pimentón* over and add enough hot water to just cover the potatoes. Add the bell peppers and bay leaf, pushing them in among the potatoes with a wooden spoon. Sprinkle with ½ teaspoon salt. Bring to a gentle simmer, reduce the heat to low, and cook, stirring occasionally, until the peppers are soft, about 15 minutes.

In a small bowl, combine the garlic and eggs and pour the mixture over the potatoes and peppers. Cook for a few minutes until the egg has set. While the egg is cooking, place a slice of bread in each of 4 shallow soup plates.

Serve the soup ladled over the bread slices.

WINE SUGGESTION: A FULL-BODIED TEMPRANILLO-BASED RED FROM EXTREMADURA

Spanish cooks have always understood the power of garlic. In this humble soup, a classic of Castilian cuisine, garlic gives substance to a dish that would otherwise be plain to the point of austerity. Like Jewish chicken soup, *sopa de ajo* is famously restorative, and efficacious for warding off colds and flu.

castilian garlic soup

1 cup (250 ml) olive oil

Six thin slices day-old country white bread (about 6 oz/170 g)

6 cloves garlic, thinly sliced

1 tablespoon finely chopped yellow onion

1 heaping teaspoon *pimentón* (Spanish smoked pepper)

6 cups (1.5 l) boiling water

1 sprig fresh flat-leaf parsley, leaves minced

6 large eggs

Fine sea salt

serves 6

Preheat the oven to 375°F (190°C).

In a frying pan, heat the olive oil over medium-high heat. Add the bread slices, in batches as needed, and fry, turning once, until golden brown. Using tongs, transfer to a flameproof, ovenproof terra-cotta casserole dish, arranging them in a single layer.

Pour out most of the oil from the frying pan and return it to medium heat. Add the garlic and onion and sauté until lightly browned, 7–8 minutes. Remove from the heat, add the *pimentón,* and stir once or twice. Pour the contents of the frying pan over the bread.

Place the casserole dish over low heat and add the boiling water and parsley. Raise the heat to medium and bring back to a boil, stirring once or twice, then simmer for 5 minutes.

Crack the eggs into the soup, sprinkling a little salt on each one. Transfer the dish to the oven and bake until the eggs are just cooked, 10–15 minutes. Serve piping hot.

COOK'S NOTE: Try adding a little chopped serrano ham along with the eggs.

WINE SUGGESTION: AN EASY-DRINKING RED FROM LA MANCHA

Chestnuts were a staple food in northern Spain for centuries, if not millennia. Nourishing and rich, they kept the wolf from the door when other harvests failed and times were hard. In recent years their sweet nuttiness has found a new role, and passed-over chestnut recipes—like this satisfying soup—are appreciated again.

chestnut soup

1 lb (500 g) fresh chestnuts, or about 10 oz (315 g) unsweetened canned or vacuum-packed chestnuts

1 large yellow onion, chopped

1 clove garlic, chopped

4 oz (125 g) serrano ham, chopped

3 oz (90 g) salt pork, chopped

Fine sea salt and freshly ground black pepper

3 tablespoons olive oil

3 tablespoons fresh lemon juice

6 thin slices coarse country bread (about 6 oz/170 g), cut in half and toasted

serves 6

If using fresh chestnuts, cut a deep cross in the flat side of each nut. Bring a saucepan three-fourths full of water to a boil, add the fresh chestnuts, and boil for 15 minutes. Drain and, while the nuts are still warm, remove the thin shell and the furry inner lining. Cut the nuts in half and return them to the saucepan. If using canned chestnuts, drain them; if using vacuum-packed chestnuts, unwrap them. Cut the nuts in half and put them in a large saucepan.

Add 6 cups (1.5 l) water, all but 3 tablespoons of the onion, the garlic, ham, salt pork, and 1 teaspoon salt to the saucepan and bring to a boil. Cover partially, reduce the heat to low, and simmer until the nuts are very soft, about 1½ hours.

In a small frying pan, heat the olive oil over medium heat. Add the 3 tablespoons onion and sauté until tender, about 8 minutes. Stir the onion into the soup. Season with salt and pepper, then stir in the lemon juice. To serve, divide the toasted bread among soup plates and ladle the hot soup over.

WINE SUGGESTION: A MINERALLY, BLACKCURRANTY GALICIAN RED FROM THE MENCÍA GRAPE

When the nights get cold on the high plains of Castile, folks get out their stockpots and boil up a *caldo*. Nothing could be more comforting than a vat of broth bubbling away for hours on the stove as the kitchen fills with its sweet, warm aroma. It makes a great base for other soups and stews, and it freezes perfectly.

spanish broth with fideo noodles

2 lb (1 kg) beef bones

½ whole chicken, preferably a stewing hen (about 1½ lb/ 750 g; see Cook's Note)

2 leeks

3 carrots

2 ribs celery

½ teaspoon black peppercorns

Fine sea salt

12 oz (375 g) Spanish *fideo* noodles or angel hair pasta

serves 6

In a large stockpot, combine the beef bones, chicken, whole leeks, carrots, and celery, and the peppercorns. Add 5 qt (5 l) water and bring to a boil, skimming off any foamy impurities. Reduce the heat to medium-low and simmer until the chicken meat is falling off the bones and the vegetables are soft and mushy, about 3 hours.

Remove the bones, meat, and vegetables and strain the broth through a cheesecloth-lined colander into a large saucepan. You should have about 3 qt (3 l) of stock. (Reserve the chicken meat for another use, if desired.)

Allow to cool thoroughly and skim off any surface fat, then slowly bring to a boil again and reduce the *caldo* further if a stronger flavor is preferred. Season with salt.

Add the *fideos* to the pot and simmer until the noodles are soft, about 4 minutes. Serve in mugs or soup bowls.

COOK'S NOTE: Spanish cooks are fond of using *gallina* (stewing hen) to give maximum flavor to soups and stews. However, a standard roasting chicken is quite permissible. My personal *caldo* ingredient list is by no means exclusive, admitting cuts of boiling beef or ham, chicken carcasses, root vegetables…

WINE SUGGESTION: A STRONG, DRY AMONTILLADO SHERRY FROM JEREZ DE LA FRONTERA (TRY ADDING A DASH TO THE BROTH)

One of the pleasures of my move to Extremadura, on the far western edge of Spain, was discovering an unexpected trove of traditional dishes—many of them as simple to make as they are delicious. This comforting tomato soup is commonly eaten with fresh figs as an accompaniment: a deft and surprising touch.

tomato soup with fresh figs

¼ cup (60 ml) olive oil

4 cloves garlic, chopped

1 yellow onion, chopped

2 green and 1 red bell peppers, seeded and broken into 1-inch (2.5-cm) pieces

6 large ripe tomatoes, peeled, seeded, and chopped

Fine sea salt and freshly ground black pepper

1 teaspoon cumin seeds, ground in a mortar and pestle

1 cup *tomate frito* (page 180) or tomato purée

2 bay leaves

1 sprig fresh flat-leaf parsley, leaves chopped

1 handful of fresh mint, leaves chopped

1 sprig *each* fresh thyme and oregano, leaves chopped (optional)

4 cups (1 l) hot water

8 thin slices country bread (about 8 oz/250 g)

8 ripe figs

serves 4

In a heavy flameproof casserole dish or Dutch oven, heat the olive oil over low heat. Add the garlic and sauté until just colored, 1–2 minutes. Using a slotted spoon, transfer to a small bowl and set aside.

Raise the heat to medium-high and add the onion and bell peppers. Sauté until the vegetables are soft, 6–7 minutes. Stir in the tomatoes, then add 1 teaspoon salt, the cumin, and the *tomate frito*. Return the garlic to the pan along with the bay leaves, parsley, mint, and thyme and oregano, if using. Cook, stirring frequently, until the vegetables are melting into one another and the mixture smells sweet, about 15 minutes.

Pour in the hot water, stir well, and simmer for 10 minutes longer. Taste and adjust the seasoning, then remove from the heat, cover, and let cool a little. Remove and discard the bay leaves.

To serve, place 2 bread slices in each of 4 bowls and ladle the soup over them. Pass around a bowl of fresh figs for guests to help themselves.

WINE SUGGESTION: A FORTHRIGHT, FRUITY ROSADO FROM NAVARRA

During the months of summer in Mallorca, this refreshing salad is ubiquitous on dining tables all over the island. Peppers, tomatoes, and onions—no lettuce or cucumber. Simplicity itself. The only question is whether you like the vegetables for *trempó* in hand-torn, rustic chunks or neatly sliced rings. (I prefer the latter.)

mallorcan summer salad

FOR THE VINAIGRETTE

2 tablespoons red or white wine vinegar

Fine sea salt and freshly ground black pepper

1/3 cup (80 ml) extra-virgin olive oil

3 large ripe tomatoes, coarsely chopped

1 thick green onion, including pale green parts, or 1 small yellow onion, thinly sliced

1 green bell pepper, seeded and cut into narrow strips or rings

1 red bell pepper, seeded and cut into narrow strips or rings

serves 4

To make the vinaigrette, in a bowl, whisk together the vinegar and 1/2 teaspoon salt. Slowly add the olive oil while whisking constantly. Taste and adjust the seasoning with salt and pepper.

Put the tomatoes, green onion, and bell peppers in a large bowl and toss to combine. Dress the salad with the vinaigrette, toss well, and serve.

WINE SUGGESTION: A SPICY, RUSTIC RED WINE FROM MALLORCA

Spain likes its salads the way it likes almost everything else: robust, colorful, and packed with flavor. This one is an anthology of punchy aromas, from salty anchovies and olives to serrano and sausage, truly a complete meal served in a salad bowl.

ensalada mixta

FOR THE VINAIGRETTE

3 tablespoons red wine vinegar

Fine sea salt and freshly ground black pepper

½ cup (125 ml) extra-virgin olive oil

2 ripe tomatoes

2 hard-boiled large eggs, peeled

8 cups torn mixed salad greens such as red-leaf romaine, escarole, and chicory

1 red onion, cut into thin rings

1 green bell pepper, seeded and cut into narrow strips

6 olive oil–packed anchovy fillets

12 oil-cured black olives

4 thin slices serrano ham

16–20 thin slices cured sausage such as salchichón, salami, chorizo, or *sobrassada*

serves 4

To make the vinaigrette, in a bowl, whisk together the vinegar and ½ teaspoon salt. Slowly add the olive oil while whisking constantly. Taste and adjust the seasoning with salt and pepper.

Quarter the tomatoes and eggs lengthwise and put them in a large bowl with the salad greens. Add the onion and bell pepper, drizzle with the vinaigrette, and toss together to mix evenly.

Pile the mixture on a large serving platter and decorate with the anchovies and olives. Tear the ham slices and arrange the ham and the sausage on and around the platter. Serve at once.

PAIRING SUGGESTION: A JUG OF ICED SANGRÍA (PAGE 183), MADE WITH WHITE WINE INSTEAD OF RED

This curious dish from my adopted home village of Hoyos, in Extremadura, must be one of the few examples in world cuisine of lemons being used for their flesh, rather than for their juice. A zingingly fresh salad that combines cooked egg yolk with lashings of olive oil for a creamy dressing, it makes the best possible partner for simply roasted or barbecued meats.

lemon mojo

Fine sea salt and freshly ground black pepper

2 medium all-purpose potatoes, peeled and cut into 1-inch (2.5-cm) dice

6 lemons, plus thin slices for garnish

1 green bell pepper, seeded and finely chopped

2 green onions, white and pale green parts, finely chopped

2 cloves garlic, minced

4 sprigs fresh flat-leaf parsley, leaves minced

3 hard-boiled large eggs, peeled

½ cup (125 ml) extra-virgin olive oil

serves 4

In a saucepan, bring 2 inches (5 cm) of salted water to a boil. Add the potatoes, reduce the heat to medium-high, and cook until just tender, 6–8 minutes. Drain and rinse in cold water until cool, then set aside.

Using a knife, peel the lemons, removing both the colorful peel and white pith. Slice alongside each segment to free it from the surrounding membrane. Coarsely chop the lemon flesh and put in a salad bowl. Add the potatoes, bell pepper, green onions, garlic, and parsley.

Cut the eggs in half lengthwise. Gently pop out the yolks and put them in a mortar and pestle. Add the olive oil and pound to create a thick sauce. Season generously with salt and pepper.

Finely chop the egg whites and add to the salad bowl. Pour the sauce over and, using wooden servers, toss carefully until all the ingredients are well combined. Garnish with thinly sliced lemon and serve at once.

WINE SUGGESTION: AN EASY-DRINKING AIRÉN WHITE FROM LA MANCHA

The stretch of coastline between Málaga and Almería is known as the Costa Tropical for its mild temperatures and all-year-round sunshine. As you drive along the coastal highway, it's easy to see mango and avocado plantations alongside the more traditional orange and almond groves. This zingy salad, a brilliant sidekick to grilled fish or shrimp, is my personal homage to a bright and beautiful corner of the Spanish Mediterranean.

orange, avocado & almond salad

5 large Valencia oranges

3 small Hass avocados

1 small red onion

⅓ cup (1½ oz/45 g) flaked almonds

FOR THE DRESSING

½ teaspoon Dijon mustard

Fine sea salt and freshly ground black pepper

1 tablespoon sherry vinegar

Juice of 1 orange (about ½ cup/125 ml)

¼ cup (60 ml) extra-virgin olive oil

serves 6

Using a knife, peel the oranges, removing both the colorful peel and white pith. Thinly slice the flesh crosswise, removing any remaining white pith, and arrange in a shallow serving dish.

Cut the avocados in half, remove the pits, and cut into ⅜-inch (1-cm) slices, discarding the peel. Slice the onion into fine rings and arrange on top of the oranges along with the avocado slices. Sprinkle with the almonds.

To make the dressing, in a small bowl, combine the mustard, a generous pinch of salt, a grinding of pepper, and the vinegar, then whisk in the orange juice. Add the oil in a thin stream as you continue to whisk.

Just before serving, whisk the dressing well and pour over the salad.

WINE SUGGESTION: A FRESH, FRUITY MEDITERRANEAN WHITE FROM ALICANTE

The genius of *xató* is the way the rich, nutty sauce combines with the salty chunks of fish and the satisfying crunch of escarole. A loaf of crusty bread is essential to mop up the delicious sauce left at the bottom of your plate.

escarole salad with salt cod, anchovies & olives

6 oz (170 g) salt cod

FOR THE SAUCE

½ cup (2 oz/60 g) blanched almonds

4 nyora or romesco peppers or ancho chiles, or 1 teaspoon *pimentón picante* (hot Spanish smoked pepper)

1 slice coarse country white bread (about 1 oz/30 g), crust removed

1 tablespoon red wine vinegar

8–10 hazelnuts

4 cloves garlic, peeled

⅓ cup (80 ml) extra-virgin olive oil

Fine sea salt

8 cured anchovy fillets

6 oz (170 g) olive oil–packed canned tuna, drained and separated into 1-inch (2.5-cm) chunks

2 ripe tomatoes, coarsely chopped

¾ cup (4 oz/125 g) small black olives such as Arbequina

1 head escarole, cored and leaves separated

serves 6

To desalt the salt cod, put it in a bowl and add cold water to cover, cover the bowl, and refrigerate for 2 days, changing the water once a day.

To make the sauce, in a dry, heavy frying pan, toast the almonds over medium heat until browned, about 30 seconds. Transfer to a plate to cool.

If using nyora peppers, soak them in boiling water for 10 minutes, then scrape the flesh off the skins.

Sprinkle the bread with the vinegar. Using a large mortar and pestle, grind together the almonds, hazelnuts, garlic, peppers, and the vinegar-soaked bread until a thick, reddish paste forms. (Alternatively, process the ingredients together in a food processor, making sure the mixture remains coarse.) Add the olive oil in a thin stream, stirring constantly with a wooden spoon, until the sauce is just liquid enough to be poured. Season with salt and set aside.

Drain the salt cod. Remove any bones and skin, then shred the meat with your fingers into thin strips. Cut or tear the anchovy fillets into strips. Put the salt cod, anchovies, and tuna in a bowl, add the tomatoes and olives, and toss to combine. Pour over enough of the sauce to coat everything thickly and toss again.

Just before serving, in a large salad bowl, toss the escarole with the salt cod mixture. Serve at once.

COOK'S NOTE: The sauce will keep in the refrigerator for 1 week. Use leftover sauce with roast meats or vegetables.

WINE SUGGESTION: A FRAGRANT, YOUNG WHITE WINE SUCH AS A SPANISH SAUVIGNON BLANC

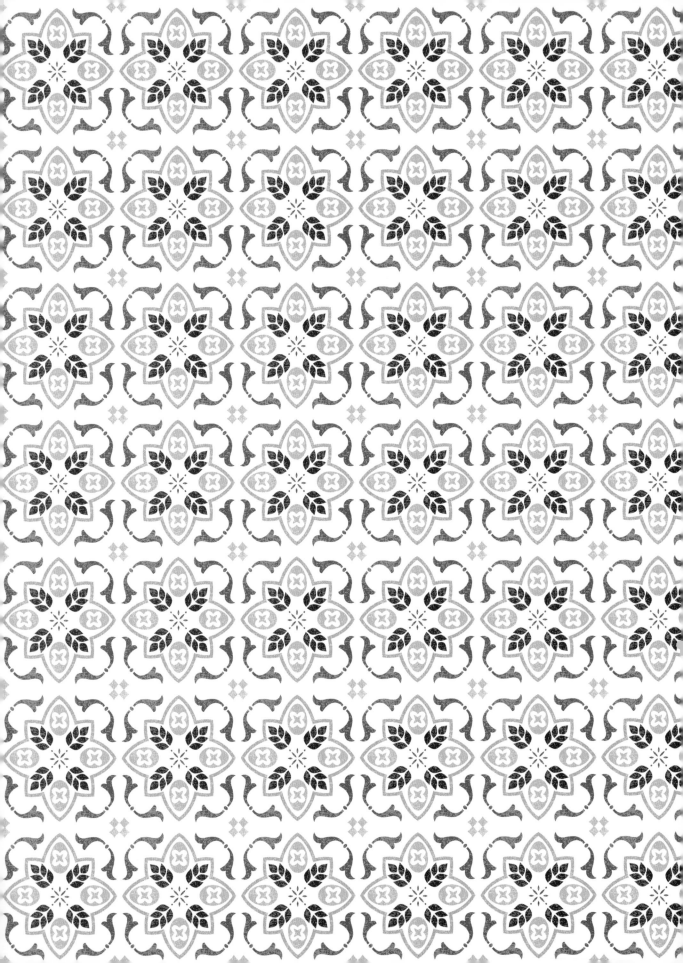

eggs, pasta, rice & more

Spain's national dish is always said to be paella, but I'd vote for *migas*. This humblest of foods was invented by the shepherds who still roam the plains of Castile with their flocks, making good use of less-than-fresh bread for a rustic meal cooked over an open fire. Nowadays *migas* ("crumbs") are a popular breakfast dish—try them as part of a hearty mid-morning brunch.

migas

1 lb (500 g) day-old country bread, crusts removed (see Cook's Note)

Fine sea salt

10 tablespoons (150 ml) olive oil

8 cloves garlic, unpeeled

7 oz (220 g) pancetta or bacon, cut into ½-inch (12-mm) dice

1 red bell pepper, seeded and chopped

1 teaspoon *pimentón* (Spanish smoked pepper)

4 large eggs

serves 4

The day before, break the bread with your fingers into roughly shaped dice of ½–1 scant inch (12 mm–2.5 cm) and spread on a tray. Sprinkle a little salted water over, cover with a kitchen towel, and let stand overnight.

In a large, wide frying pan, heat 2 tablespoons of the oil over high heat. Add the unpeeled garlic cloves and the pancetta and fry until the pancetta is crisp and browned, about 2 minutes. Using a slotted spoon, transfer to a bowl. Add the bell pepper to the pan and fry until beginning to blister, about 2 minutes. Transfer to the bowl with the garlic and pancetta.

Add 6 tablespoons olive oil to the pan. Have ready 1 cup (250 ml) water. When the oil is hot, add the bread pieces, tossing them quickly in the oil and using your fingers to sprinkle them with water from time to time. The aim is to ensure the *migas* achieve a uniform golden brown without burning or drying excessively. Finally, return the garlic, pancetta, and bell pepper to the pan and season with ½ teaspoon salt and the *pimentón*. Toss everything together until combined, 1–2 minutes. Turn out onto a serving platter.

In a small nonstick frying pan, heat the remaining 2 tablespoons olive oil over medium heat. Fry the eggs one by one until cooked to your liking. Serve the *migas* with the fried eggs on top.

COOK'S NOTE: The bread used for *migas* shouldn't be fresh, but not quite hard either—somewhere in between.

WINE SUGGESTION: A RICH, VELVET-SMOOTH GARNACHA FROM THE D.O. VINOS DE MADRID

This dish, called *pisto manchego* in Spanish, evolved from an ancient stew called *alboronia*, Moorish for "eggplant." The original stew is thought to have included Arabic seasonings such as cumin, saffron, and cilantro. Over time, vegetables from the New World were introduced into the mix, as this recipe illustrates.

summer vegetable stew with eggs

2 large eggplants, about 1½ lb (750 g) total weight

Fine sea salt and freshly ground black pepper

¾ cup (180 ml) olive oil

2 large yellow onions, chopped

1 lb (500 g) bell peppers, a mixture of red and green, seeded and chopped

½ cup (2½ oz/75 g) unbleached all-purpose flour

2 lb (1 kg) tomatoes, peeled, seeded, and diced

1 teaspoon dried oregano

6 eggs

2 tablespoons pine nuts, toasted

serves 6

Peel the eggplants and cut into 1½-inch (4-cm) pieces. Place in a colander, sprinkling salt between the layers, and let drain for 1 hour.

In a large frying pan over medium heat, heat ¼ cup (60 ml) of the olive oil. Add the onions and sauté until tender, 8–10 minutes. Add the peppers and sauté until softened, about 5 minutes longer.

Meanwhile, rinse the eggplant pieces and pat dry. Place the flour in a shallow bowl. In another large frying pan over high heat, heat the remaining ½ cup (120 ml) oil. Dip the eggplant pieces in the flour, tapping off the excess. In batches, add to the hot oil and fry, turning as needed, until golden, 5–8 minutes. Using a slotted spoon, transfer to a plate.

When all of the eggplant pieces have been fried, add them to the onion-pepper mixture along with the tomatoes, oregano, and salt and pepper to taste. Reduce the heat to low and simmer until the flavors are well blended and the tomatoes have broken down into a saucelike consistency, about 20 minutes.

Using the back of a large spoon, make 6 indentations in the vegetable mixture and break an egg into each one. Sprinkle with salt and pepper. Cover the pan and cook until the whites of the eggs have set but the yolks are still runny, 6–8 minutes.

Garnish with pine nuts and serve, using a large spoon to dish out portions of *pisto* topped with an egg.

WINE SUGGESTION: AN OAKED RED FROM LA MANCHA, LIKE SEÑORIO DE LOS LLANOS RESERVA

I first encountered these "married" eggs at the house of a friend, where they were a favorite family supper dish. Hard-boiled eggs are first stuffed, then battered, then briefly simmered for a dish that is somehow much more than the sum of its parts. A marriage made in heaven?

huevos casados

6 hard-boiled eggs

3½ oz (105 g) *ibérico* or serrano ham, finely chopped

2 tablespoons whole milk

Oil for deep frying

1 tablespoon flour

1 beaten egg

2 cloves garlic, peeled and left whole

1 sprig fresh flat-leaf parsley, leaves chopped

1 cup (8 fl oz/250 ml) chicken or vegetable stock, preferably homemade (page 178)

1 bay leaf

Fine sea salt and freshly ground black pepper

Nutmeg

Crusty bread for serving

serves 6

Peel the hard-boiled eggs and slice in half lengthwise. Take out the yolks and place them in a small bowl with the chopped ham and the milk, mixing gently with a fork to combine thoroughly. Use this mixture to stuff the egg whites, aiming for a rounded shape as the filling protrudes from the cavity.

In a frying pan over medium-high heat, heat 2 inches (5 cm) of oil until hot, but not smoking. One by one, coat each egg half first in flour, then in beaten egg. Deep-fry each until the batter is golden, about 3 minutes. Remove with a slotted spoon to a warmed platter.

In the same oil, fry the 2 garlic cloves until just colored, then place in a mortar and pestle and grind to a paste with the parsley. Turn off the heat and cover the pan.

In a small, heavy casserole dish (choose one in which the eggs will fit snugly), bring the stock to a simmer, then mix in the garlic and parsley paste and add the bay leaf. Season well with a little salt, pepper, and freshly grated nutmeg to taste. Place the battered eggs in the pan cut-side up, cover, and simmer over low heat for 5 minutes.

Serve with crusty bread to mop up the juices.

WINE SUGGESTION: A FRUITY, REFRESHING ROSADO FROM NAVARRA

It's a common sight in the wintertime in Spain: a figure by the road-side carrying a stick and a plastic bag, hunting for wild asparagus. Like some of the best Spanish dishes, this *revuelto* ("scramble") is almost embarrassingly simple, but it shines when prepared with the best possible ingredients—such as fresh farm eggs.

scrambled eggs with asparagus

2 bunches (about 1 lb/500 g) green asparagus, tough ends trimmed

Fine sea salt and freshly ground black pepper

2 tablespoons olive oil

6 eggs

2 cloves garlic, finely chopped

serves 4

Separate the asparagus stalks from the tips and cut the stalks into 1-inch (2.5-cm) pieces.

In a heavy omelet pan or sauté pan, bring to a boil a little salted water and simmer the asparagus stalk pieces for 3 minutes. Then add the tips and simmer for another minute. Drain and set aside.

Pat the same pan dry and place over low heat, then add the olive oil.

Beat the eggs with a fork and season them with salt and pepper.

Stir-fry the parcooked asparagus for a few seconds, add the garlic, and sauté briefly until lightly colored. Pour in the beaten egg and allow to cook for 20 seconds. Drag a wooden spoon through the egg and asparagus mixture a few times until the egg is just cooked and the *revuelto* has a creamy (not dry) texture. Turn off the heat and turn out into a serving dish.

COOK'S NOTE: If you can find it, the most ideal asparagus for this dish is the slender and slightly bitter wild kind (also called "sprue").

WINE SUGGESTION: AN OLD-FASHIONED, FULL-BODIED WHITE RIOJA LIKE MARQUÉS DE MURRIETA

Legend has it this dish was invented in a bar in Seville, where the customers thought it so gaudy and colorful they compared it to a flamenco dancer—hence its Spanish name, *huevos a la flamenca*. A freewheeling mélange, the dish readily admits other seasonal vegetables, including spring asparagus tips, summertime zucchini, and autumn butternut squash.

flamenco-style eggs

FOR THE MIGAS

4 thick slices day-old country bread

Olive oil for frying

2 cloves garlic, crushed slightly

Fine sea salt and freshly ground black pepper

Pimentón dulce **(sweet Spanish smoked pepper)**

2 tablespoons olive oil

4 oz (125 g) pancetta, diced

2 Spanish-style semicured chorizo sausages, diced

1 yellow onion, chopped

2 cloves garlic, minced

2 red bell peppers, seeded and chopped

1 cup fresh or thawed frozen peas

1 lb (500 g) fresh tomatoes, chopped, or 1 can (14 oz/ 400 g) diced tomatoes

Pimentón picante **(hot Spanish smoked pepper)**

Fino sherry, as needed

8 eggs

3 tablespoons chopped fresh flat-leaf parsley

serves 4

Preheat the oven to 350°F (180°C). Warm 4 individual-size earthenware baking dishes or ramekins.

To make the *migas,* cut the crusts off the stale bread and blitz in a food processor (or use a hand grater) to make crumbs.

In a large frying pan over high heat, heat a generous glug of olive oil. Add the garlic cloves and cook for a minute to flavor the oil (do not let the garlic burn), then remove and discard. Add the crumbs to the pan and brown them quickly, stirring and shaking the pan, and scooping them out onto paper towels with a slotted spoon. Season the *migas* with a little salt, pepper, and *pimentón.* Set the *migas* aside.

Wipe out the frying pan, place over medium heat, and add the oil. Add the pancetta and chorizo and fry until they start to render their fat. Add the onion and garlic and cook gently, stirring, until softened, about 8 minutes. Add the peppers, peas, and tomatoes and cook, stirring occasionally, until softened and thickened, about 10 minutes. Add *pimentón* to taste and a splash of sherry to keep the mixture moist.

Divide the vegetable mixture among the warmed baking dishes. Break 2 eggs over each baking dish. It does not matter if a yolk breaks.

Bake the eggs and vegetables until the eggs are just set, 8–10 minutes. Sprinkle the *migas* around the edges of each dish, garnish with the parsley, and serve warm.

PAIRING SUGGESTION: A SANGRÍA (SEE PAGE 183) MADE WITH RED WINE, SODA, CHOPPED FRUIT, PLENTY OF ICE, AND A SLUG OF SPANISH BRANDY

After a hard morning's work in the vegetable patch, this rustic fry of eggs and potatoes, fragrant with garlic and sweet red pepper, is my quick and calorific lunch of choice. For those not lucky enough (like me) to have their own hens, it's absolutely worth tracking down some really good organic free-range eggs at your local farmers' market.

mixed fry of egg, potato, pepper & garlic

2 cups (500 ml) olive oil

8 cloves garlic, crushed

2 lb (1 kg) potatoes, peeled and thinly sliced

1 large red bell pepper, seeded and cut into 1-inch (2.5-cm) pieces

Fine sea salt and freshly ground black pepper

8 eggs

serves 4

In a wide, deep frying pan over high heat, heat the oil.

Add the garlic cloves and fry until light golden brown in color. Remove and reserve. Add the potato slices and fry for 5 minutes, then add the bell pepper and fry until the potatoes are browned and the pepper soft and sweet, 5–6 minutes more.

Remove from the heat and ladle out most of the oil from the pan. Return the pan to medium heat and add the garlic. Season well with salt and pepper. Using a spatula or skimmer, make 8 small spaces in the potato and red pepper mixture and break an egg directly into each one. When the whites are almost set, flip the eggs with their surrounding vegetables to form a series of roughly shaped patties. Cook for a few seconds more, then turn off the heat.

Serve straight from the pan.

WINE SUGGESTION: A RUSTIC GARNACHA-BASED RED FROM ARAGÓN'S D.O. CAMPO DE BORJA

The Spanish word *tortilla*, "little cake," was used for this potato omelet and other similar dishes long before it was adopted for flatbread in the New World. Making the potatoes properly tender and creamy for this dish requires poaching them slowly in olive oil.

tortilla española

1 cup (250 ml) olive oil, plus 2 tablespoons

2 lb (1 kg) waxy potatoes, peeled and cut into slices ¼ inch (6 mm) thick

Fine sea salt and freshly ground black pepper

1 yellow onion, thinly sliced

1 leek, white part only, thinly sliced

6 large eggs

serves 6–8

In a large frying pan over medium-low heat, heat the 1 cup (250 ml) olive oil. Add half of the potatoes, season with salt and pepper, and fry, turning occasionally, until the slices are tender but not browned, 15–20 minutes. Using a slotted spatula or spoon, transfer the potatoes to a colander placed over a bowl. Repeat with the remaining potatoes. Leave the oil in the pan.

In another frying pan over medium heat, heat the 2 tablespoons olive oil. Add the onion and leek and cook, stirring often, until the onion is soft and the leek tender, about 12 minutes. Set aside to cool slightly.

In a large bowl, whisk the eggs until well blended. Using a slotted spoon, add the onion and leek. Fold in the cooked potatoes. Let stand for 5 minutes to allow the potatoes to absorb some of the egg.

Pour off all but ⅓ cup (80 ml) of the oil from the large frying pan and place it over low heat. Pour in the vegetable-egg mixture. Cook until the bottom of the omelet is set and golden brown, 8–10 minutes, shaking the pan regularly to avoid sticking. Invert a large round platter on top of the pan, invert the pan and plate together, and lift off the pan. Slide the omelet back into the pan and return it to low heat. Cook until the second side is set, about 4 minutes.

Invert the tortilla again onto a plate. Wipe away any smears of oil from the edge of the plate with paper towels. Let it stand until slightly cooled, at least 10 minutes. Cut into pieces and serve hot or at room temperature.

WINE SUGGESTION: A RICHLY FRUITY, VELVETY RIBERA DEL DUERO

Everybody loves rice with lobster—there's even a Spanish website devoted to it. Rich and unctuous, tasting of the sea, with an intense stock that permeates the rice while leaving lots of concentrated sauce, this lobster-based treat is the perfect example of an *arroz caldoso* ("soupy rice"). By way of accompaniment, a simple green salad is all that's needed.

rice with lobster

8 cups (64 fl oz/2 l) fish stock, preferably homemade (page 178)

1 lb (500 g) small shrimp in the shell

Fine sea salt

1 large live lobster

3 tablespoons olive oil

1 small red onion, finely chopped

3 canned piquillo peppers or 1 red bell pepper, seeded and finely chopped

1 plum tomato, peeled and minced (or grated)

6 sprigs fresh flat-leaf parsley, leaves minced

Generous pinch of saffron

2 tablespoons good-quality brandy

1 cup (7 oz/220 g) short-grain Spanish rice such as Bomba or Calasparra

1 teaspoon *pimentón* (Spanish smoked pepper)

serves 2

In a pot, heat the stock over medium heat. Add the shrimp and simmer for 10 minutes. Transfer the stock and shrimp to a food processor or blender and liquidize. Strain the stock through a fine-mesh sieve. Season to taste with salt, cover to keep warm, and set aside.

Using a large, sharp knife, cut the lobster into 6 serving pieces: make 2 cuts, lengthwise and across the body, then cut off the claws and crack them once. (More tender-hearted readers can put the lobster in the freezer for a few minutes to put it to sleep before cutting it up.)

In a heavy (preferably cast-iron) flameproof casserole dish or Dutch oven, heat the olive oil over medium-high heat. Add the lobster pieces and cook, turning occasionally, until browned. Using tongs, transfer to a large bowl.

Add the onion and peppers to the casserole dish. (If you are using fresh bell pepper, fry it first until soft and caramelizing, about 3 minutes.) Reduce the heat to medium and sauté until the vegetables are soft. Stir in the tomato, parsley, and saffron and cook until a rich-smelling *sofrito* has formed, about 3 minutes.

Add the brandy and simmer until the alcohol has evaporated, about 30 seconds.

Add the rice, stir until coated with oil, and sprinkle with the *pimentón*. Nestle the lobster pieces into the rice and pour in the stock. Bring to a boil and simmer, uncovered, for 10 minutes, then reduce the heat to very low and cook until the rice is tender, about 8 minutes longer (depending how soupy you like it). Remove from the heat and let cool for about 5 minutes.

Serve the rice with lobster directly from the casserole dish at the table.

WINE SUGGESTION: A SMOOTH, FULL-BODIED SPANISH CHARDONNAY

Arroz a banda (meaning "rice on the side") is an iconic specialty of Catalan coastal cuisine. Fish and potatoes are simmered in an enriched broth flavored with *pimentón de la Vera*, Spain's favorite spice, made from ground smoked peppers. The fish and potatoes are then kept warm while the broth is used to prepare a paella-style rice.

arroz a banda

¼ teaspoon saffron threads

3 tablespoons slivered blanched almonds

1 clove garlic, chopped

2 tablespoons fresh flat-leaf parsley leaves

2 tablespoons fresh lemon juice

1 tablespoon *pimentón* (Spanish smoked pepper)

6 cups (48 fl oz/1.5 l) fish stock, preferably homemade (page 178)

Fine sea salt and freshly ground black pepper

1 lb (500 g) small red or yellow potatoes, cut into 2-inch (5-cm) pieces

1½ lb (750 g) firm-fleshed white fish fillets

2 tablespoons olive oil

⅔ cup (4 oz/125 g) canned crushed tomatoes

2 cups (14 oz/400 g) short-grain Spanish rice such as Bomba or Calasparra

In a small, dry frying pan, toast the saffron threads over medium heat, stirring constantly or shaking the pan, until fragrant and a shade darker, about 1 minute. Pour the threads into a bowl and, when cool, crumble with your fingertips. Set aside.

In a blender or food processor, combine the almonds, garlic, and parsley and blitz until finely chopped. Add the lemon juice and *pimentón* and process to a smooth paste.

In a large pot, bring the stock to a boil over medium-high heat. Stir in the almond mixture, breaking it up with a fork so it dissolves. Season well with salt and pepper and reduce the heat to maintain a brisk simmer. Add the potatoes, cover, and cook for 12 minutes. While the potatoes are cooking, cut the fish into 4–6 equal pieces. Add the fish to the pot with the potatoes and cook, uncovered, until the fish flakes easily when cut with a fork and the potatoes are tender, 8–10 minutes longer. Using a slotted spoon, gently transfer the fish and potatoes to a platter and cover to keep warm. Measure the broth and add water if needed to total 5 cups (1.25 l); set aside.

In a 14-inch (35-cm) paella pan or a large frying pan with sides 2 inches (5 cm) high, heat the olive oil and tomatoes together over medium heat. Stir in the saffron and cook, stirring frequently, until the tomato solids have cooked down into a rough paste, about 5 minutes. Add the reserved broth and bring to a boil.

Sprinkle the rice evenly over the bottom of the pan. Raise the heat to medium-high and bring to boil. Cook for 10 minutes. Reduce the heat to low and continue to cook until the liquid has been absorbed and the rice is tender, about 10 minutes longer. Remove from the heat, cover with aluminum foil, and let stand for 10 minutes.

FOR THE GARLIC
MAYONNAISE

1 clove garlic, chopped

1 large egg

**1 tablespoon fresh
lemon juice**

**1 tablespoon fresh flat-leaf
parsley leaves**

Fine sea salt

¾ cup (180 ml) olive oil

serves 4–6

Meanwhile, make the garlic mayonnaise. In a blender or food processor, combine the garlic, egg, lemon juice, parsley, and ¼ teaspoon salt and whizz until smooth. With the motor running, pour in the olive oil in a slow, steady stream and process until a thick mayonnaise forms. Scrape into a bowl. (The sauce can be made a day ahead, covered, and refrigerated.)

Serve the rice directly from the pan. Serve the fish and potatoes at the same time or after the rice. Pass the garlic mayonnaise at the table.

WINE SUGGESTION: A SMOOTH, AROMATIC WHITE FROM THE SOUTH OF SPAIN, MADE FROM THE PALOMINO FINA GRAPE

Murcia, on the southeast coast of Mediterranean Spain, is a major agricultural region and a place where vegetables are the true aristocrats of the kitchen. This vibrantly colored rice dish makes a welcome change from the more common fish- and/or meat-based true paellas, not to mention a treat for vegans.

vegetable "paella"

¾ cup (180 ml) olive oil

1 green bell pepper, seeded and cut into 1½-inch (4-cm) pieces

5 oz (155 g) broccoli, cut into florets

5 oz (155 g) cauliflower, cut into florets

5 oz (155 g) shelled, blanched, and peeled fava beans (fresh or frozen)

5 oz (155 g) green beans, trimmed

3 cloves garlic, thinly sliced

5 oz (155 g) peas (fresh or frozen)

1¼ cups (310 ml) *tomate frito* (page 180) or tomato purée

9 cups (72 fl oz/2.25 l) vegetable stock, preferably homemade (page 178)

Fine sea salt

2 cups (14 oz/400 g) rice

Lemon wedges for serving

serves 6

In a 15-inch (38-cm) paella pan (see Cook's Note) or large frying pan with sides 2 inches (5 cm) high, heat the olive oil over medium-high heat. Add the bell pepper, broccoli, cauliflower, fava beans, and green beans and sauté until the cauliflower is lightly browned, about 5 minutes.

Add the garlic and peas and sauté for 30 seconds longer (do not let the garlic burn).

Pour in the *tomate frito* and the stock and add 1 tablespoon salt. Bring to a simmer and add the rice, stirring to mix everything well and evenly distribute the vegetables.

Reduce the heat to very low and simmer very gently without stirring until the rice is a little more than al dente, about 20 minutes.

Remove the pan from the heat, cover with aluminum foil, and let stand for 5–10 minutes (during this time the rice will absorb any remaining liquid).

Serve with a bowl of lemon wedges for guests to squeeze over the rice.

COOK'S NOTE: Paella pans can be bought in Spanish specialty food stores as well as in specialized kitchen supply stores or online. If you can't find one, a very wide, deep frying pan may do almost as well.

WINE SUGGESTION: A FRUITY, FRESH CHARDONNAY-BASED WHITE FROM THE PENEDÈS, LIKE MIGUEL TORRES' VIÑA SOL

This dramatic-looking dish can be found all along the Spanish Mediterranean coast, from the French border to the Straits of Gibraltar. Though freshly caught squid comes with its own ink sac, to obtain a good black color you'll need to add extra squid or cuttlefish ink—sold in packets at high-end fish markets.

seafood with black rice

1 lb (500 g) whole squid

1 lb (500 g) live mussels, scrubbed and debearded

1¼ cups (310 ml) olive oil

2 yellow onions, chopped

2 green bell peppers, seeded and finely chopped

3 or 4 cloves garlic, minced

1 cup (6 oz/170 g) peeled, seeded, and chopped tomato (fresh or canned)

5 cups (1.25 l) water or fish stock (page 178), or as needed

2 cups (14 oz/400 g) short-grain Spanish rice such as Bomba or Calasparra

1–2 tablespoons squid or cuttlefish ink

16 jumbo shrimp or a mixture of crayfish and shrimp, in the shell

Fine sea salt and freshly ground black pepper

Allioli (page 180) for serving

serves 4–6

To clean each squid, pull the head and clinging innards free from the body. Discard the innards, reserving the ink sac. Cut the fins, tentacles, and arms from the head and squeeze out the hard beak from the mouth at the base of the tentacles. Pull out and discard the transparent quill-like cartilage from the body pouch. Rinse out the body and rub off the mottled violet skin covering it, then rinse the tentacles. Leave the tentacles whole. Cut the bodies into rings ½ inch (12 mm) wide. Set aside.

Place the mussels in a deep frying pan, discarding any that do not close to the touch. Add ½ cup (125 ml) water, cover, and place over high heat. Cook, shaking the pan occasionally, until the mussels open, about 5 minutes. Using a slotted spoon, transfer the mussels to a bowl, discarding any that failed to open. Pour the cooking liquid through a fine-mesh sieve lined with cheesecloth placed over the bowl of mussels. Set aside.

In a 12-inch (30-cm) paella pan or a large, deep frying pan, heat half of the olive oil over medium heat. Add the onions, bell peppers, and garlic and sauté until tender, about 10 minutes. Add the tomato and sauté until it releases its liquid, a few minutes longer. Add about 1 cup (250 ml) of the water or fish stock and simmer for 20 minutes to blend the flavors. Add the rice, the remaining 4 cups (1 l) water or stock or as needed to cover, and 1 tablespoon squid ink. Simmer over medium heat until the rice has absorbed about half of the liquid, about 10 minutes.

Meanwhile, in a frying pan, heat the remaining olive oil over high heat. Add the shrimp and sauté until they turn pink and begin to curl, 2–3 minutes. Remove from the heat and season with salt and pepper. Add the shrimp, cooked mussels and their juices, and the squid to the rice. If the rice is not as dark as you would like, add the remaining squid ink. Reduce the heat to low and simmer until the rice is cooked through, 10–15 minutes longer. Transfer to a platter and serve at once, dolloped with *allioli*.

WINE SUGGESTION: A VIBRANT RED LIKE TINTO ROBLE

Many versions of paella exist, and this one has become one of the most popular and well known, but it's far from traditional. In Valencia, birthplace of paella, the dish might include duck, rabbit, snails, and seasonal vegetables like romano beans. This mixture strikes a nice balance between ancient and modern.

chicken & shellfish paella

¼ teaspoon saffron threads

1½ lb (750 g) chicken legs and thighs

Fine sea salt and freshly ground black pepper

2 tablespoons olive oil

1 yellow onion, finely chopped

1 clove garlic, minced

⅔ cup (160 ml) *tomate frito* (page 180) or tomato purée

½ cup (125 ml) dry white wine

5 cups (40 fl oz/1.25 l) chicken stock, preferably homemade (page 178)

1 teaspoon *pimentón* (Spanish smoked pepper)

2 cups (14 oz/400 g) short-grain Spanish rice such as Bomba or Calasparra

12 live clams, scrubbed

12 live mussels, scrubbed and debearded

12 large shrimp, peeled and deveined

½ cup (3 oz/90 g) roasted red bell pepper strips

½ cup (2½ oz/75 g) fresh or thawed frozen peas

3 lemons, quartered

serves 6–8

In a small, dry frying pan, toast the saffron threads over medium heat, stirring constantly or shaking the pan, until fragrant and a shade darker, about 1 minute. Pour the threads into a bowl and, when cool, crumble with your fingertips. Set aside.

Halve the chicken pieces across the bone with poultry shears. Season the chicken generously with salt and pepper. In a 14-inch (35-cm) paella pan or a 12-inch (30-cm) frying pan with sides 2 inches (5 cm) high, heat the olive oil over medium heat. Working in batches without crowding, add the chicken and cook, turning as needed, until nicely browned on all sides, about 5 minutes. Transfer to a plate.

Add the onion and garlic to the pan and sauté until softened, about 5 minutes. Add the *tomate frito* and cook, stirring, until most of the liquid has evaporated, 3–5 minutes. Add the wine, stock, *pimentón,* and saffron, then season to taste with salt and pepper. Bring to a boil.

Sprinkle the rice evenly over the bottom of the pan, then arrange the chicken over the rice, submerging it in the liquid. Raise the heat to high and bring to a boil, then cook for 10 minutes.

Arrange the clams, mussels, and shrimp over the rice, discarding any clams or mussels that do not close to the touch. Push the seafood down into the liquid. Reduce the heat to low and simmer until the clams and mussels have opened (discard any that fail to open), the shrimp are pink, and the liquid has been absorbed, 10–12 minutes. Using a wooden spoon, push aside the rice to see if there is a nice brown crust on the bottom of the pan. If one hasn't formed yet, cook for a few minutes longer, adjusting the heat as necessary to brown, but not burn, the rice.

Remove from the heat. Arrange the bell pepper strips and peas over the rice, cover with aluminum foil, and let stand for 10 minutes. Serve at once directly from the pan, with the lemon wedges for diners to squeeze over.

WINE SUGGESTION: A FRUIT-PACKED, HERB-SCENTED MEDITERRANEAN RED FROM D.O. VALENCIA, SUCH AS LES ALCUSSES

The town of Elche, in Alicante province, is famous for two things: one, the medieval mystery play performed every year over two days in August; and two, the town's signature dish, a kind of paella of mixed meats and rice with a thin crust of beaten egg. It is highly savory and lovely to look at, emerging from the oven with a golden yellow crust puffed up slightly around the meat, legume, and rice filling.

rice with chicken, sausage & chickpeas

6 oz (170 g) ground pork

1 cup (2 oz/60 g) fresh bread crumbs

Fine sea salt and freshly ground black pepper

½ cup (2 oz/60 g) dried bread crumbs

2 *each* chicken thighs and rabbit or chicken legs

½ cup (125 ml) olive oil, plus 2 tablespoons

⅓ lb (155 g) fresh pork sausages, cut into 2-inch (5-cm) pieces

1 teaspoon saffron threads

Leaves from 3 fresh flat-leaf parsley sprigs

In a bowl, mix the pork with the fresh bread crumbs and season well with salt and pepper. Form into little balls about the size of small walnuts, then roll the meatballs in the dried bread crumbs. Set aside.

Halve the thighs and legs across the bone with poultry shears and season with salt and pepper. In a flameproof, ovenproof ceramic casserole dish or a Dutch oven, heat the ½ cup (125 ml) olive oil over medium heat. Add the chicken and, if using, the rabbit and cook, turning as needed, until browned on all sides, about 6 minutes. Using a slotted spoon, transfer to a plate and set aside, reserving the remaining oil in the casserole.

Return the casserole to medium heat and add the sausage pieces. Fry until nicely browned, about 4 minutes. Using the slotted spoon, transfer to paper towels to drain, reserving the remaining oil in the casserole.

Preheat the oven to 425°F (220°C). In a frying pan, heat the 2 tablespoons olive oil over medium heat. Add the meatballs and fry, turning, until golden brown, about 5 minutes. Using the slotted spoon, transfer to a small roasting pan or baking dish and bake until cooked through, about 10 minutes more. Keep the oven set at 425°F (220°C).

Using a mortar and pestle, grind together 1 teaspoon salt and the saffron threads until a deep yellow powder forms. Add the parsley and grind together to form a thick paste. Set aside.

6 cloves garlic, lightly
crushed

1⅓ cups (9 oz/280 g)
short-grain Spanish rice such
as Bomba or Calasparra

1 large tomato, peeled and
chopped

1 qt (32 fl oz/1 l) chicken
stock, preferably homemade
(page 178), heated

¾ cup (5 oz/155 g) canned
chickpeas, drained and
rinsed

4 large eggs

serves 4

Preheat the oven to 425°F (220°C). Return the casserole dish and reserved oil to medium-high heat, add the garlic, and sauté until soft, about 2 minutes. (This may seem a large amount of garlic, but it is used only to flavor the oil.) Using the slotted spoon, remove and discard the garlic.

Add the rice to the casserole and sauté in the hot oil for about 30 seconds, then add the tomato and stir for 30 seconds longer. Add 3 cups (750 ml) of the stock, the saffron-parsley mixture, the chicken and rabbit pieces, and the sausage. Reduce the heat to medium and cook without stirring until all the liquid has been absorbed, 12–15 minutes. Test the rice; the grains should be tender but not entirely soft. If further cooking is necessary, add a little more stock as needed. Remove from the heat and arrange the chickpeas and meatballs on top of the rice.

In a small bowl, whisk the eggs until blended and pour them evenly over the rice. Immediately transfer to the oven and bake until the egg crust is opaque and beginning to brown, about 10 minutes. Remove from the oven and let cool slightly before serving.

WINE SUGGESTION: A ROBUST, FULL-BODIED RED WINE FROM THE D.O. ALICANTE

Newcomers to Spanish cuisine are often surprised that a dish similar to paella is made, not with rice, but with pasta—or to be precise, with *fideos*, a Spanish take on noodles. This dish, hailing from the seaside town of Gandía, is supposed to have been invented by a fisherman who ran out of rice on board his boat.

spanish noodles with fish, clams & shrimp

¼ teaspoon saffron threads

3 tablespoons olive oil

1 yellow onion, finely chopped

½ cup (2½ oz/75 g) seeded and chopped green bell pepper

1 tablespoon minced garlic

3½–4 cups (28–32 fl oz/ 875 ml–1 l) fish or chicken stock, preferably homemade (page 178)

1 lb (500 g) ripe tomatoes, grated, or 1 cup (6 oz/170 g) canned crushed tomatoes

½ cup (125 ml) dry white wine

1½ teaspoons *pimentón* (Spanish smoked pepper)

Fine sea salt and freshly ground black pepper

12 oz (375 g) Spanish *fideo* noodles or angel hair pasta, broken in half or in pieces

12 oz (375 g) halibut or other white fish fillets, cut into 1-inch (2.5-cm) pieces

½ lb (250 g) live clams, scrubbed

½ lb (250 g) shrimp, peeled and deveined

3 tablespoons chopped fresh flat-leaf parsley

serves 4

In a small, dry frying pan, toast the saffron threads over medium heat, stirring constantly or shaking the pan, until fragrant and a shade darker, about 1 minute. Pour the threads into a bowl and, when cool, crumble with your fingertips. Set aside.

In a 12-inch (30-cm) paella pan or a large, deep frying pan, heat the olive oil over medium-high heat. Add the onion, bell pepper, and garlic and sauté until the vegetables are soft, 3–5 minutes. Add 3½ cups (875 ml) of the stock, the tomatoes, wine, *pimentón,* and saffron and stir to combine. Season to taste with salt and pepper. Stir in the noodles.

Bring to a boil over medium-high heat and cook for 8 minutes. Adjust the heat to maintain a gentle simmer and add ½ cup (125 ml) more stock if the mixture looks dry. Add the halibut and clams, discarding any clams that do not close to the touch. Push the fish down into the liquid. Cover and cook for 5 minutes. Add the shrimp, cover, and cook until the clams have opened (discard any that fail to open), the shrimp are pink, and most of the liquid has been absorbed, 3–5 minutes longer.

Remove from the heat and let stand, covered, for 10 minutes. Sprinkle with the parsley, spoon into bowls, and serve at once.

COOK'S NOTE: This dish is traditionally served with *allioli* (page 180).

WINE SUGGESTION: A FRUIT-PACKED, PINK-COLORED ROSADO FROM NAVARRA

Italian food is much admired in Spain, but Spanish versions of Italian dishes are not as common as you might expect. This original take on ravioli, invented by chef Antonio Navarro (who is married to an Italian), must be the exception that proves the rule.

ravioli stuffed with torta del casar cheese

FOR THE DOUGH

2 large eggs plus 1 large egg yolk

Fine sea salt

1¾ cups (9 oz/280 g) unbleached all-purpose flour, plus more for dusting

FOR THE FILLING

7 oz (220 g) *Torta del Casar* cheese (see Cook's Note)

1 large egg yolk

1½ tablespoons unsalted butter, at room temperature

1 large egg, beaten

To make the pasta, beat together the eggs and egg yolk with a pinch of salt. Put the flour in a large bowl, making a well in the center. Add the beaten eggs to the well and stir them into the flour with a fork, then mix with your hands into a smooth, elastic dough. Cover with plastic wrap and let rest in the fridge for 15 minutes.

To make the filling, in a small bowl, beat the cheese with the egg yolk and butter until thoroughly combined.

Dust a work surface with flour. Divide the dough into two halves and roll each out with a rolling pin into a 10-inch (25-cm) square about ⅛ inch (3 mm) thick. Using a ruler and the back of a knife, mark out the ravioli bases on one of the dough squares: four vertical and four horizontal lines, equally spaced, will make a total of 25 ravioli bases.

Spoon the filling into a piping bag. Pipe a level teaspoon of filling at the center of each raviolo base.

Brush around the edge of each raviolo base with beaten egg. Place the second dough square on top of the first. Using a serrated pasta cutter, cut out the ravioli and press gently around the edge of each to seal. Transfer the ravioli to a clean kitchen towel and let stand in a cool place for 1 hour.

Bring a large pot of salted water to boil. Drop the ravioli into the pot one by one and simmer until the pasta is tender, 3–5 minutes. Drain and transfer to a serving dish.

FOR THE SAUCE

2 tablespoons butter

4 fresh sage leaves

½ cup (125 ml) heavy cream

½ cup (4 fl oz/125 ml) chicken stock, preferably homemade (page 178)

Freshly grated Parmigiano-Reggiano cheese for serving

serves 4

To make the sauce, in a small, heavy saucepan, melt the butter over medium-high heat and fry the sage leaves for a few seconds. Add the cream and stock and simmer until creamy and slightly reduced.

Spoon the sauce over the ravioli. Serve with Parmigiano-Reggiano.

COOK'S NOTE: The stuffing is based on the sheep's milk cheese *Torta del Casar.* To open the cheese, cut round the edge of the rind, open it like a lid, and spoon out the cheese. If you can't find *Torta,* another gooey, bloomy-rind cheese (like Camembert) might do almost as well.

WINE SUGGESTION: A FULL-BODIED RED FROM THE TEMPRANILLO GRAPE (TRY D.O. RIBERA DEL GUADIANA)

seafood, poultry & meat

This preparation is from the region of Navarra, whose mountain rivers are known for their trout. Here, serrano ham is tucked into the cavities and imparts its sweetness to the fish. Accompany with roast or boiled potatoes tossed with olive oil, chopped fresh parsley, and sea salt.

trout stuffed with ham

4 whole boned trout, about 8 oz (250 g) each (see Cook's Note)

3 tablespoons olive oil

Fine sea salt and freshly ground black pepper

1 teaspoon sherry vinegar or red wine vinegar

4 thin slices serrano ham

12 sprigs fresh thyme

serves 4

Preheat the oven to 425°F (220°C).

Rinse the trout and pat dry with paper towels. Rub the skin and cavity of each fish with the olive oil. Sprinkle each cavity lightly with salt and pepper and drizzle each with ¼ teaspoon of the vinegar. Arrange the trout in a single layer in a roasting pan.

Tuck 1 slice of ham and 3 thyme sprigs lengthwise in the cavity of each trout and fold over to close.

Roast the trout until the skins are crisp and the flesh flakes easily with a fork, 10–12 minutes. Transfer to individual plates and remove the thyme sprigs. Serve at once.

COOK'S NOTE: You will need to buy whole boned trout for this dish, or buy bone-in trout (they should weigh about 12 oz/375 g each) and bone them yourself.

WINE SUGGESTION: A NAVARRESE CHARDONNAY

Jon Warren is a young Englishman whose company San Sebastián Food offers visitors a fast-track experience of Basque food and culture. It was in one of Jon's cookery courses, at the legendary Hotel Maria Cristina, that I picked up the recipe for this classic dish featuring Spain's favorite fish: the much undervalued hake.

white fish & clams in salsa verde

½ cup (2½ oz/75 g) unbleached all-purpose flour

Fine sea salt and freshly ground black pepper

6 thick (3-inch/7.5-cm) hake steaks (about 2 lb/ 1 kg total weight), cut across the backbone (see Cook's Note)

2 tablespoons olive oil

1 clove garlic

1-inch (2.5-cm) length of red chile

¾ cup (180 ml) dry white wine

2 cups (16 fl oz/500 ml) fish stock, preferably homemade (page 178)

12 live littleneck clams, scrubbed

6 white asparagus spears, tough ends trimmed (see Cook's Note)

4 oz (125 g) fresh or thawed frozen baby peas

1 small bunch (about 12 sprigs) fresh flat-leaf parsley, leaves chopped

serves 4–6

Put the flour in a shallow bowl and season with salt and pepper. Lightly dredge the fish on both sides, shaking off any excess flour.

In a wide, heavy sauté pan, heat the oil over medium heat. Add the garlic clove and chile and fry gently until the garlic is just beginning to color, 1–2 minutes. Using a slotted spoon, remove and discard the garlic and chile.

Place the hake pieces one by one in the pan, moving each one gently as it makes contact with the oil to prevent sticking. Fry until just browned, then turn carefully to brown the other side. Transfer to a plate.

Raise the heat to medium-high, pour the wine into the pan, and stir to scrape up any browned bits from the pan bottom. Pour in the stock and simmer, stirring, for 1–2 minutes. Add the clams, discarding any that do not close to the touch, and cook until they open, discarding any that remain closed. Using a slotted spoon, transfer the clams to the plate with the hake.

Add the asparagus and peas to the pan and simmer until the asparagus is tender, about 5 minutes. Add the parsley. Return the hake and clams to the pan, cover, and simmer until the fish is just cooked through, 3–5 minutes.

Arrange the hake pieces, clams, and vegetables on a serving dish and spoon the sauce over.

COOK'S NOTE: If you can't find hake, cod or flounder make decent substitutes. If you can find tender stems of fresh white asparagus, use them. If not, jarred white asparagus makes an acceptable substitute—as does fresh green asparagus.

WINE SUGGESTION: A CRISP, STEELY-FRESH TXAKOLI WHITE FROM THE BASQUE COUNTRY

Swordfish is a great fish for cutting into thick steaks, the only drawback being its tendency to dry out during cooking. In this recipe, inspired by one originating up the coast in neighboring Portugal, the steaks roast in the oven along with a rich sauce of onion, tomato, anchovy, and olive oil. If swordfish isn't available, thick fillets of cod or sea bass will do fine.

swordfish steaks with tomatoes & anchovies

5 tablespoons (80 ml) olive oil, plus more for greasing

6 swordfish steaks, about 7 oz (220 g) each

Fine sea salt and freshly ground black pepper

1 yellow onion, chopped

2 cups (12 oz/375 g) peeled, seeded, and chopped plum tomatoes

1 tablespoon finely minced cured anchovy fillets

2 tablespoons tomato paste dissolved in ¼ cup (60 ml) dry white wine

20 black olives, pitted and coarsely chopped

¼ cup (⅓ oz/10 g) chopped fresh flat-leaf parsley, plus more for garnish

Lemon wedges for serving

serves 6

Preheat the oven to 400°F (200°C). Oil a baking dish large enough to hold the fish steaks in a single layer.

Sprinkle the fish with salt and pepper. In a large frying pan, heat the olive oil over medium heat. Add the onion and sauté until tender, about 8 minutes. Add the tomatoes, anchovies, tomato paste mixture, olives, and parsley and simmer until thickened, about 5 minutes.

Place the fish steaks in the prepared baking dish. Spoon the tomato sauce over the fish. Roast until the fish is opaque throughout, about 15 minutes.

Remove from the oven and sprinkle with parsley. Serve at once directly from the dish, accompanied with lemon wedges.

WINE SUGGESTION: AN AROMATIC, APPLE-FRESH WHITE GODELLO FROM D.O. VALDEORRAS, IN GALICIA

Packing a whole fish in rock salt is one of the best ways to cook it, and the technique is found in all the countries bordering the Mediterranean. The salt keeps the flesh moist and brings out the flavor of the fish, while the skin locks out intense saltiness. The whole fish emerging from its salty tomb is a spectacle in itself.

sea bass in a salt crust

Butter for greasing

1 whole dorada, red snapper, or other firm-fleshed fish, about 3 lb (1.5 kg), cleaned and scaled by the fishmonger

4 lb (2 kg) rock salt

Freshly ground black pepper

1 lemon, cut into wedges

Allioli (page 180) for serving (optional)

serves 4

Preheat the oven to 475°F (245°C).

Butter a baking dish large enough to hold the fish comfortably. Place the fish in the prepared baking dish and cover evenly and completely with the rock salt. Roast until the salt has formed a hard crust, about 45 minutes.

Using a large stainless-steel spoon, remove as much of the salt as possible. Carefully skin and fillet the fish, then transfer the fillets to individual plates.

Season with a generous grinding of pepper. Serve with the lemon wedges and, if desired, *allioli.*

WINE SUGGESTION: A FRAGRANT, FRUITY WHITE ALBARIÑO FROM GALICIA OR A PENEDÈS WHITE

The name of this famous Barcelona dish, *bacallà a la llauna*, refers to salt cod, a traditional Spanish ingredient that is still much enjoyed, especially during the season of Lent when meat is officially off the menu. The dish is even better (as well as easier) with fresh cod, as made in this recipe.

baked cod with olive oil & garlic

½ cup (2½ oz/75 g)
unbleached all-purpose flour

Fine sea salt and freshly
ground black pepper

2 lb (1 kg) fresh cod fillets

½ cup (125 ml) olive oil

6 cloves garlic, thinly sliced

1 tablespoon *pimentón*
(Spanish smoked pepper)

½ cup (125 ml) white wine

serves 4–6

Preheat the oven to 375°F (190°C).

Put the flour in a shallow bowl and season with salt and pepper. Lightly dredge the cod fillets on both sides, shaking off any excess flour.

In a frying pan, heat the oil over medium-high heat. Add the cod fillets and fry until golden brown. Transfer to a small roasting pan, leaving the oil in the hot pan.

Add the garlic to the frying pan and fry until just colored, about 1 minute (do not allow the garlic to burn). Remove from the heat and stir in the *pimentón*. Add the wine, return the pan to medium-high heat, and simmer, stirring occasionally, for 3 minutes.

Pour the wine mixture over the fish. Roast in the oven until the fish is just cooked through, about 10 minutes. Serve at once.

WINE SUGGESTION: ACCORDING TO SPANISH CUSTOM, COD IS OFTEN MATCHED WITH A RED WINE—TRY AN AROMATIC, MINERAL-RICH GARNACHA FROM PRIORAT OR MONSANT

Along with bell peppers, eggplants, and turkey, the squid is one of nature's most obvious candidates for stuffing. The tubular, pocket-like shape of the *calamar* simply cries out for a tasty filling. This time-honored recipe is one of many Catalan versions of stuffed squid, but it wins out in authenticity as well as sheer deliciousness.

catalan-style stuffed squid

1 lb (500 g) whole squid
(see Cook's Note)

6 tablespoons (90 ml)
olive oil

2 yellow onions,
finely chopped

1 lb (500 g) ground pork

1 hard-boiled large egg,
peeled and finely chopped

2 tablespoons pine nuts

Fine sea salt and freshly
ground black pepper

3 tablespoons flour

3 tomatoes, peeled and
minced (or grated)

½ cup (125 ml) white wine

½ cup (125 ml) fish stock
or clam juice if needed

FOR THE PICADA

2 cloves garlic

¼ cup (1 oz/30 g) raw
blanched almonds

Leaves from 6 sprigs
fresh flat-leaf parsley

Crusty bread for serving

serves 4

To clean each squid, pull the head and clinging innards free from the body and discard. Cut the fins, tentacles, and arms from the head and squeeze out the small, hard beak from the mouth at the base of the tentacles. Pull out and discard the transparent quill-like cartilage from the body pouch. Rinse out the body and rub off the mottled violet skin covering it. Finely chop the tentacles, arms, and fins. Set aside.

In a heavy frying pan, heat 3 tablespoons of the olive oil over medium-high heat. Add half of the chopped onions, the pork, and the chopped squid and sauté until lightly browned, about 10 minutes. Add the hard-boiled egg and pine nuts and simmer until any liquid has boiled away and the mixture is nearly dry, about 5 minutes more. Season well with salt and pepper. Remove from the heat and let cool.

Using a funnel and the handle of a wooden spoon, stuff the pork mixture into the squid bodies, closing each one with a toothpick. The filling should be well packed into the squid, but not bursting out of the opening.

Put the flour in a small bowl and dredge each squid in the flour, shaking off any excess flour (only a light dusting is required).

In a wide, heavy flameproof casserole dish with a lid, heat the remaining 3 tablespoons olive oil over medium heat. Add the squid and brown on both sides. Using a slotted spoon, transfer to a plate and set aside.

In the same oil (pick out any burned bits before proceeding), sauté the remaining onion over medium-high heat until translucent, about 3 minutes. Add the tomatoes and cook, stirring with a wooden spoon, until the vegetables have combined into a sweet-smelling sauce, about 5 minutes more. Pour in the wine and bubble until the alcohol has burned off, about 30 seconds. Season the sauce with a little salt and pepper.

continued

Place the squid in the sauce, reduce the heat to medium-low, cover, and simmer gently for about 10 minutes, shaking the pan from time to time to prevent sticking and adding a little fish stock if needed.

Meanwhile, make the *picada.* In a mortar and pestle, pound together the garlic, almonds, and parsley. Alternatively, whizz in a food processor or blender to a coarse texture. Sprinkle the *picada* over the squid, shaking the pan to incorporate, and simmer gently for 5 minutes more.

Bring the squid to the table in the casserole dish and serve with plenty of crusty bread.

COOK'S NOTE: Squid come in many sizes, the best for this recipe being on the small side, about 4 inches (10 cm) long. This recipe is designed for about 16 squid of this size; the larger the squid, the fewer you will need, obviously.

WINE SUGGESTION: A BIG, JUICY RED FROM THE RIBERA DEL DUERO

The Spanish region of Galicia is in love with octopus and enjoys its *pulpo* most of all simply boiled and dressed with olive oil, salt, and *pimentón*—with the optional addition of potatoes. Galician octopus is invariably served on a rimmed wooden plate; look for one in Spanish speciality food shops, or use a chopping board.

octopus with potatoes

Sea salt

1 octopus, weighing about 3 lb (1.35 kg) (see Cook's Note)

3 medium all-purpose potatoes, about 1½ lb (750 g) total weight

Flaky sea salt

1 teaspoon *pimentón* (Spanish smoked pepper)

¼ cup (60 ml) top-quality extra-virgin olive oil

serves 4

Bring a large pot of salted water to a boil over medium-high heat, add the whole (frozen) octopus, and boil until soft, about 1 hour. (Test the thickest part of the tentacles with a sharp knife: the tip should penetrate easily.) Remove the octopus from the pot and drain thoroughly in a colander, reserving the cooking liquid.

Peel the potatoes and cut into ½-inch (12-mm) slices. Add to the octopus cooking liquid and simmer gently over medium heat until just tender. Drain and lay the slices on a rimmed wooden plate or cutting board.

Using poultry shears or kitchen scissors, cut the octopus tentacles into 1-inch (2.5-cm) chunks. Discard the head. Arrange the octopus chunks on top of the potatoes. Sprinkle with 1 teaspoon flaky sea salt and the *pimentón,* then drizzle with the olive oil. Serve warm.

COOK'S NOTE: Octopus is naturally tough and rubbery, and needs to be softened before cooking. In the past, this was done by beating the octopus against a rock; nowadays, the same result is achieved by freezing and defrosting. Since most octopus are sold frozen anyway, there is no need for any further action. Do ensure, however, that your prefrozen octopus has not also been precooked.

WINE SUGGESTION: AN AROMATIC, FLOWERY ALBARIÑO FROM D.O. RIAS BAIXAS

Christmas in Murcia wouldn't be the same without these delicate meatballs, made with turkey meat—traditionally from a female bird made tipsy with wine before being dispatched!—and hauntingly flavored with lemon zest, garlic, and pine nuts. Simmered in a saffron-scented chicken stock, they certainly give the standard holiday roast turkey a run for its money.

turkey & pine nut meatballs in saffron broth

1 cup (2 oz/60 g) fresh brown bread crumbs

¼ cup (60 ml) whole milk

1 lemon

1¼ lb (625 g) ground turkey breast meat

8 oz (250 g) lean ground pork

8 oz (250 g) pancetta or bacon, minced

2 large eggs, beaten

3 tablespoons pine nuts

2 cloves garlic, minced

1 handful fresh flat-leaf parsley, leaves minced

Fine sea salt and freshly ground white pepper

FOR THE BROTH

6 cups (48 fl oz/1.5 l) chicken stock, preferably homemade (page 178)

Generous pinch of saffron threads

serves 4

In a shallow bowl, soak the bread crumbs in the milk for 2 minutes.

Grate the zest from the lemon and set aside. Cut the zested lemon in half and set aside.

In a large bowl, using your hands, combine the turkey, pork, pancetta, soaked crumbs, eggs, pine nuts, garlic, and parsley. Add the lemon zest and season generously with salt and white pepper. Mix thoroughly.

To make the broth, in a large saucepan, combine the stock and saffron threads. Place over medium-high heat and simmer gently until the stock has taken on a golden saffron color, about 5 minutes.

Meanwhile, make the meatballs. Keeping the lemon halves within reach, form the mixture into balls slightly larger than a ping-pong ball, squeezing a little lemon juice on your hands for ease of handling.

Reduce the heat under the broth to very low. Using a large slotted spoon, carefully lower the meatballs into the broth, working in batches of 5–6 or as many as will fit in the pan without touching each other. Simmer each batch very gently for 10–12 minutes, then transfer to a serving dish. Finally, strain the stock and pour it over the meatballs just before serving.

WINE SUGGESTION: A FRUITY, JUICY SYRAH FROM D.O. MONTSANT

A classic country dish, *pollo al ajillo* is less often seen on Spanish menus than it used to be. I would say it is high time for a revival. The juicy chunks of fried chicken, the roasty sweetness of garlic, and the heady fragrance of fino sherry add up to an irresistible combination. Use a good grain-fed chicken (organic, if possible).

chicken cooked with garlic

1 grain-fed chicken, about 4 lb (1.8 kg), breast and backbone removed, cut across the bone in walnut-sized pieces (ask your butcher to do this for you)

Fine sea salt and freshly ground black pepper

1 head garlic

1 cup (250 ml) olive oil

¾ cup (180 ml) dry fino sherry

1 dash sherry vinegar or other white wine vinegar

Handful of fresh flat-leaf parsley, leaves finely chopped

serves 2–4

Reserve the chicken breasts for another recipe, as they tend to dry out excessively. Place the dark chicken meat chunks in a large bowl and season generously with salt and pepper, turning to ensure the chunks are evenly coated.

Separate the garlic cloves, without peeling, and crush them whole with the blade of a large knife.

In a wide, deep frying pan, heat the olive oil over medium-high heat. When hot, add the garlic cloves and fry until they are beginning to take on a light golden color, about 1 minute. Using a slotted spoon, transfer to a bowl.

Add the chicken to the pan and fry until the chunks are golden brown, 5–10 minutes. Pour or ladle off the excess oil and reserve for another use (it will be great for frying potatoes). Return the garlic cloves to the pan and pour in the sherry. Bubble until a thick sauce has formed, turning the chicken chunks in the wine as it reduces. Add the dash of vinegar and stir to combine. Remove from the heat, sprinkle with the parsley, and turn out into a serving dish.

COOK'S NOTE: Serve with a bowl of green olives and a basket of crusty bread.

WINE SUGGESTION: AN AROMATIC, BRACING FINO SHERRY

Andalucía is known for its bitter Seville oranges, which are the classic ingredient in orange marmalade and in the golden sauce for this braised duck. If you can't find bitter oranges, navel oranges may be used instead. Keeping the peel on one of the oranges gives the dish its distinctive, slightly bitter citrus taste.

duck with olives, sherry & orange

2 Seville or navel oranges, preferably organic

1 duck, about 5 lb (2.5 kg), cut into 4 pieces, excess skin, fat, and wing tips removed

Fine sea salt and freshly ground black pepper

1 tablespoon unsalted butter

1 large yellow onion, chopped

2 tablespoons flour

½ cup (125 ml) fruity white wine

½ cup (125 ml) dry fino sherry

2 carrots, chopped

1 tablespoon chopped fresh flat-leaf parsley

1 tablespoon fresh thyme leaves

1 bay leaf

1 cup (5 oz/155 g) green olives, each olive cracked into 3–5 pieces

serves 4

Using a sharp knife, cut a slice off both ends of each orange to reveal the flesh. Cut 1 orange crosswise into slices ¼ inch (6 mm) thick. Place the second orange upright on the cutting board. Using the knife, cut downward to remove the colorful peel and white pith, following the contour of the fruit. Cut crosswise into slices ¼ inch (6 mm) thick. Set the oranges aside.

Pierce the duck pieces all over with a fork. Season both sides generously with salt and pepper. In a large, heavy frying pan, melt the butter over medium heat. Add the duck pieces and cook, turning as needed, until browned on all sides, about 15 minutes total. Transfer the duck to a platter. Pour off all but 1 tablespoon of the fat from the pan.

Return the pan to medium-high heat. Add the onion and cook, stirring often, until golden, 5–7 minutes. Add the flour and cook, stirring, for 1 minute. Pour in the wine, sherry, and 1 cup (250 ml) water and stir to scrape up any browned bits from the pan bottom. Return the duck to the pan, along with any accumulated juices. Add the carrots, parsley, thyme, bay leaf, oranges, and 2 cups (500 ml) water and bring to a boil. Reduce the heat to medium-low, cover, and simmer very gently until the duck is tender, about 45 minutes. Transfer the duck to a serving platter and set the pan aside. Cover the duck with aluminum foil and let rest for 10 minutes.

Bring a saucepan three-fourths full of water to a boil. Add the olives and blanch for 3 minutes, then drain and cool under cold running water.

Skim as much fat as possible from the sauce in the pan. Remove and discard the bay leaf. If the sauce seems thin, bring to a boil for 1–2 minutes, stirring once or twice, just until thick enough to coat the back of a spoon. Reduce the heat to low and stir in the olives. Cook, stirring, until heated through. Season to taste with salt and pepper.

Spoon the sauce over the duck and serve at once.

WINE SUGGESTION: A FRESH, YOUNG, UNOAKED RED RIOJA

"Si, señor, es un buen pollo tomatero," said my neighbor, as he watched a fat chicken pick its way across the yard. For days I wondered what he had meant by "a good tomato chicken"—until I discovered this classic home-style Spanish dish. I like it best on a summer night, with fries, salad, and a big jug of iced sangría.

chicken in tomato sauce

1 small roasting chicken, about 2¾ lb (1.25 kg)

Fine sea salt and freshly ground black pepper

1 cup (250 ml) olive oil

1 large Italian frying pepper (see Cook's Note) or green bell pepper, seeded and quartered.

4 cups (1 l) *tomate frito* (page 180) or tomato purée

2 cloves garlic, minced

1 bay leaf

2 sprigs fresh oregano, leaves minced

½–1 teaspoon cayenne pepper

serves 4

Cut the chicken across the bone into large chunks (about 4 inches/10 cm), discarding the neck and spine (or, simmer these up into an impromptu stock with carrots, leek, and celery). Season the chicken chunks with salt and pepper.

In a cast-iron casserole dish with a lid or a Dutch oven, heat the olive oil over medium heat. Add the green pepper and fry until the skin is beginning to blister, about 3 minutes. Using a slotted spoon, transfer the pepper to a bowl and set aside.

Add the chicken chunks to the pan, first the dark meat (which will take 10–15 minutes) and finishing with the breast (3 minutes). Fry gently until golden brown and almost cooked through. Remove with a slotted spoon and drain on paper towels.

Pour off the oil from the pan and return the pan to medium-high heat. Add the *tomate frito* and bring to a simmer, then add the garlic, bay leaf, oregano, and cayenne pepper to taste. Season with salt. Reduce the heat, cover, and simmer for 5 minutes, stirring often.

Return the chicken chunks to the pan, stir, cover, and simmer until the meat is thoroughly cooked, about 10 minutes, stirring occasionally and adding a little water if the sauce seems too thick. Remove and discard the bay leaf before serving.

COOK'S NOTE: If available, use a long, pointed, thin-fleshed green pepper—this type is best for frying.

WINE SUGGESTION: A SANGRÍA (SEE PAGE 183) MADE WITH RED WINE, ORANGE AND LEMON JUICE, SPANISH GASEOSA OR OTHER FIZZY SODA, CHOPPED FRUIT, MINT, AND PLENTY OF ICE

My brother-in-law Enrique is one of the best cooks I know. During his regular stays at my farmhouse, I am happy to relinquish the kitchen as "Quique" cooks up a storm of down-home Spanish dishes like this rustic fry of farm-bred rabbit, aromatic with garlic and herbs and—its masterstroke—a splash of sherry vinegar.

rabbit with potatoes & garlic

1 young rabbit, about 1½ lb (750 g), meat cut into 2-inch (5-cm) pieces (ask your butcher to do this for you)

Fine sea salt and freshly ground black pepper

Leaves from 1 sprig fresh rosemary

Leaves from 2–3 sprigs fresh thyme

4 cups (1 l) olive oil

6 large cloves garlic, unpeeled, plus 2 cloves, peeled and roughly chopped

2 bay leaves

½ cup (125 ml) sherry vinegar or other white wine vinegar

1½ lb (750 g) all-purpose potatoes, peeled and cut into slices ¼ inch (6 mm) thick

serves 4–6

Place the rabbit pieces in a large bowl, season generously with salt and pepper, and add the rosemary and thyme leaves. Mix well, cover with plastic wrap, and let stand in a cool place for 30 minutes.

In a wide, high-sided frying pan, slowly heat the olive oil over low heat. Using the heel of your hand and the side of a large kitchen knife, flatten the garlic cloves, but do not crush them completely. Add to the pan as the oil is heating and cook until the garlic has browned (do not let it burn). Using a slotted spoon transfer the garlic cloves to a small bowl.

Tear the bay leaves into 1-inch (2.5-cm) pieces, stripping away the hard central rib. In a mortar and pestle, pound together the chopped garlic, bay leaf pieces (which won't disintegrate completely), and a pinch of salt. Add the vinegar and stir well.

Raise the heat to medium, add the rabbit to the pan, and gently sauté until golden brown, 10–15 minutes. Using a slotted spoon, transfer to a plate.

Raise the heat to high, add the potatoes to the pan, and fry until golden brown. Remove the pan from the heat and remove the excess oil with a ladle (in economical Spanish style, this oil can be strained and reused).

Return the rabbit and reserved whole garlic cloves to the pan and place over medium heat. Pour the vinegar-garlic mixture over the rabbit and potatoes and turn them in the sauce until most of the liquid has evaporated.

Bring the rabbit and potatoes to the table in the pan, or turn out into a serving dish.

WINE SUGGESTION: A RICHLY FLAVORED, VELVETY RED FROM D.O. RIBERA DEL DUERO

Aragon, the Spanish region that rubs up against Catalunya, is a major producer of stone fruit—apricots, nectarines, and peaches. Plantations of the local peach variety, with its evocative perfume and rich golden flesh, flourish here. This recipe matchmakes the sweetness of peach with the mild savoriness of tender pork loin.

pork chops with peaches

1 cup (5 oz/155 g) unbleached all-purpose flour

Fine sea salt and freshly ground black pepper

4 boneless pork loin chops, each about ¾ inch (2 cm) thick (about 1 lb/500 g total weight)

⅓ cup (80 ml) olive oil, or as needed

½ cup (125 ml) good-quality brandy

1 yellow onion, chopped

2 tomatoes, peeled, seeded, and chopped

2 cups (16 fl oz/500 ml) chicken stock, preferably homemade (page 178), or as needed

¾ cup (180 ml) peach nectar

3 peaches, about 1 lb (500 g) total, peeled (see Peaches in Red Wine, page 158)

serves 4

Put the flour in a shallow bowl, season with salt and pepper, and lightly dredge the pork chops on both sides, shaking off any excess flour.

In a heavy frying pan, heat the olive oil over medium heat. Add the pork and cook, turning once, until golden brown, about 3 minutes on each side. Using tongs, transfer the pork to a warmed flameproof ceramic casserole, and set aside away from the heat. Reserve the pan with the remaining oil.

In a small saucepan, heat the brandy over low heat, about 15 seconds. Pour over the pork. Use a long kitchen match to ignite the brandy. When the alcohol has burned off, the flames will die out. (Keep a pan lid ready in case the flames flare up.)

In the reserved frying pan, make a *sofregit*. Heat the oil remaining in the pan over medium heat (add a little more olive oil if needed). Add the onion and sauté until softened, about 3 minutes. Add the tomatoes and cook until they have darkened in color, 2–3 minutes. Add the stock and peach nectar, and season to taste with salt and pepper. Raise the heat to high and bring to a boil, then reduce the heat to medium-low and simmer until the sauce begins to thicken, 2–3 minutes. Pour over the pork chops, place the casserole over medium heat, and cook until the pork is just cooked through, about 30 minutes.

Meanwhile, cut each peach in half through the stem end, remove the pit, and cut into wedges.

Add the peaches to the casserole, spooning a bit of the sauce over them. Cook, adding a little more stock if necessary, until the peaches are soft but not falling apart, about 7 minutes longer.

Arrange the pork chops on a shallow serving platter and place the peaches around them. Spoon the sauce over the top and serve.

WINE SUGGESTION: A FRUITY, YOUNG RED WINE FROM THE PENEDÈS

Big in medieval times, the combination of savory with sweet has once again found favor with the Spanish palate, and even the humblest restaurant now thinks nothing of serving up goat cheese with tomato jam or pork with blackberry sauce. This is one of the best sweet-savory combos I have come across, and can be whipped up in a matter of minutes as a no-sweat main course for guests.

pork tenderloin with port wine & prunes

24 pitted prunes

1 cup (250 ml) ruby port

2 pork tenderloins

Fine sea salt and freshly ground black pepper

3 tablespoons olive oil

2 cups (16 fl oz/500 ml) ham stock (page 179) or vegetable stock (page 178)

serves 4–6

Cut each prune lengthwise into 3 or 4 strips. Place in a bowl, mix with the port, and let macerate for 1 hour.

Cut the pork tenderloins crosswise into 2-inch (5-cm) medallions. Season generously with salt and pepper.

In a wide, heavy sauté pan, heat the oil over medium heat. Add the pork medallions and cook, turning once, until browned on both sides, about 2 minutes per side, shaking the pan regularly to prevent sticking. Using tongs, transfer to a platter and set aside.

Drain the prunes, pouring the unabsorbed port into the pan. Stir to scrape up any browned bits from the pan bottom. Add the stock and simmer until the liquid has reduced by half.

Return the pork medallions to the pan and simmer over medium heat for 5 minutes. Turn them in the sauce, add the prunes, and cook until the sauce is bubbling and sticky.

Arrange the pork medallions on a serving platter, top with the prunes, and pour the sauce over.

WINE SUGGESTION: A MUSCULAR YOUNG RED TASTING OF BLACK-BERRIES, MULBERRIES, AND RASPBERRIES FROM D.O. RIBERA DEL DUERO

Though it contains just three basic ingredients—pork ribs, potato, and onion—this country stew is an example of the way traditional Spanish cooking transforms even the simplest combinations into something more than the sum of their parts. Richly savory, it's my dish of choice to feed a hungry crowd on a cold winter's day.

pork rib & potato stew

2 tablespoons olive oil

2 lb (1 kg) baby back ribs, about 4 inches (10 cm) in length, sliced into individual riblets

2 large red onions, coarsely chopped

6 cloves garlic, crushed and roughly chopped

3 lb (1.5 kg) potatoes, peeled and thickly sliced

Boiling water as needed

1 tablespoon *pimentón* (Spanish smoked pepper)

Fine sea salt and freshly ground black pepper

serves 8

In a deep cast-iron stockpot or Dutch oven, heat the olive oil over medium heat. Add the pork ribs and fry until just beginning to brown. Using tongs, transfer to a platter and set aside.

Add the onions and garlic to the pot and sauté until soft and translucent, 7–8 minutes. Return the ribs to the pot along with the potatoes. Add enough boiling water to cover, stir in the *pimentón,* and season generously with salt and pepper. Bring to a boil, then reduce the heat and simmer gently for about 1 hour. Toward the end of the cooking time, use a fork to crush a few potato pieces against the side of the pot and stir in to thicken the sauce.

Transfer to a platter or shallow bowl, and serve.

COOK'S NOTE: This stew is even better made the day before and reheated just before serving. Accompany with crusty bread and a mixed salad.

WINE SUGGESTION: A VELVETY, FULL-BODIED RED FROM THE RIBERA DEL DUERO

Sausages and beans pair up in many Western cuisines, and this is Catalunya's very own version—a favorite prepared at least once a week in households all across the region. Note that a dish as hearty and heavy as this would rarely be served in the evening, as Spaniards in general have a horror of nighttime indigestion.

fresh pork sausages with white beans & allioli

1 lb (500 g) dried cannellini beans, soaked overnight, then drained

1 large yellow onion, cut in half

2 carrots, trimmed

1 bay leaf

1 leek, white and pale green parts

¼ cup (60 ml) olive oil

1 lb (500 g) fresh pork sausages

2 cloves garlic, minced

Fine sea salt and freshly ground black pepper

Allioli (page 180) for serving

serves 4

In a large, heavy saucepan, combine the beans with 5 cups (1.25 l) cold water and the onion, 1 of the carrots, and the bay leaf. Bring to a boil, skimming off any foam that appears on the surface, and reduce the heat to simmer gently until the beans are thoroughly tender, about 1½ hours. (They should not dry out entirely—add a little more water if needed to keep them moist.)

Finely chop the remaining carrot and the leek. Set aside.

In a wide, heavy casserole dish with a lid, heat 2 tablespoons of the olive oil over medium heat. Add the sausages, pricking them to prevent bursting, and fry until browned all over and cooked through, 10–12 minutes. Using tongs, transfer to a plate and cover to keep warm.

In the casserole dish, heat the remaining 2 tablespoons olive oil over medium-high heat. Add the carrot and leek and sauté, stirring often, until beginning to brown, about 4 minutes. Add the garlic and sauté for 30 seconds more. Add ½ cup (125 ml) water, stir, and simmer until the vegetables are soft, about 6 minutes. Tip in the beans, season with 1 tablespoon salt and plenty of pepper, and mix well. Cover the pan and cook over medium heat for a few minutes to let the flavors combine.

Cut the sausages into manageable lengths and arrange over the beans in a shallow serving dish. Serve the *allioli* in a separate bowl.

WINE SUGGESTION: A POWERFUL, FLAVORFUL RED FROM D.O. TORO

It's a little-known fact that many bullrings in Spain have a butcher's shop attached where fans can buy meat from the brave bulls they have just seen perform in the ring. Fighting bull's tails are not easy to come by abroad, but the good news is that oxtail makes a fine substitute. Long, slow cooking is the key to this simple but sensational dish.

braised oxtails

⅓ cup (2 oz/60 g) unbleached all-purpose flour

Fine sea salt and freshly ground black pepper

3 lb (1.5 kg) oxtail or bull's tail, cut across the bone into thick steaks (ask your butcher to do this for you)

6 tablespoons olive oil

1 large leek, white and pale green parts, chopped

1 red bell pepper, seeded and chopped

1 large yellow onion, chopped

3 carrots, sliced

2 cloves garlic, roughly chopped

2 bay leaves

1 sprig fresh rosemary

2 sprigs fresh oregano

3 cups (750 ml) dry red wine, preferably a deep-colored Spanish red

2 cups (16 fl oz/500 ml) beef stock, preferably homemade (page 179), or as needed

serves 6

Put the flour in a shallow bowl and season with salt and pepper. Lightly dredge the meat on both sides, shaking off any excess flour.

In a cast-iron casserole dish with a lid or a Dutch oven, heat the olive oil over medium-low heat. Working in batches, brown the meat on all sides. Using tongs, transfer the meat to a plate. Add the leek, bell pepper, onion, carrots, and garlic to the pot and gently sauté until the vegetables are soft, 10–15 minutes. Add the bay leaves, rosemary, and oregano and season well with salt and pepper.

Return the meat to the pot, pour in the wine and enough stock to just cover the meat, and bring to a boil. Skim the surface for foamy impurities, then cover, reduce the heat to very low, and simmer for 3–4 hours, stirring once every hour. The meat should be so tender that it literally falls off the bone. (Alternatively, braise in a 250°F/120°C oven for the same amount of time.) Remove and discard the bay leaves and herb sprigs and serve directly from the pot.

COOK'S NOTE: Accompany with mashed or French fried potatoes and a green salad.

WINE SUGGESTION: A BIG-BODIED RED FROM D.O. TORO

Despite having a great deal in common, Spain and its neighbor Portugal were always said to live "back to back," with little cross-border exchange. This has changed, and the two countries are growing ever more curious about each other's culture and cuisine. I discovered this appealing recipe in Trás-os-Montes, not far from my home near the Portuguese border.

leg of lamb with mint & garlic

1 leg of lamb, 5–6 lb
(2.5–3 kg), boned

¾ cup (1 oz/30 g) chopped
fresh mint, plus small
leaves for garnish

¼ cup (1½ oz/45 g) finely
minced bacon

2 tablespoons minced garlic

1 tablespoon *pimentón*
(Spanish smoked pepper)

Fine sea salt and freshly
ground black pepper

5 tablespoons (75 ml)
red wine vinegar

½ cup (125 ml) olive oil

serves 6–8

Unroll the leg of lamb, fat side down, and trim away all excess fat and sinews. In a mortar or small bowl, combine the mint, bacon, garlic, *pimentón,* 1 teaspoon salt, ½ teaspoon pepper, and 2 tablespoons of the vinegar and mix to form a paste. Rub the paste evenly over the inside of the lamb leg. Roll up the leg and tie securely with kitchen string. Wrap the lamb in plastic wrap and refrigerate for 12–24 hours.

Unwrap the lamb and bring to room temperature. Preheat the oven to 400°F (200°C).

Put the lamb on a rack in a roasting pan. In a small bowl, stir together the olive oil and the remaining 3 tablespoons vinegar. Brush the lamb lightly with some of the mixture. Sprinkle with salt and pepper.

Roast, basting with the oil-vinegar mixture every 8–10 minutes, until an instant-read thermometer inserted into the thickest part registers 120°F (49°C) for rare, 45–50 minutes, or 130–135°F (54–57°C) for medium, 55–60 minutes. Alternatively, test by cutting into the lamb with a sharp knife; the meat should be rosy or done to your liking.

Transfer the lamb to a carving board and let rest for 10 minutes. Snip the strings and slice to serve. Garnish with fresh mint leaves.

WINE SUGGESTION: A PORTUGUESE RED FROM THE DOURO VALLEY

The mushrooms most commonly used for *fricandó*, a rich, dark, and flavorful beef stew, are *moixernons* (commonly known in English as "St. George's mushrooms")—small and unassuming to look at but giving off a heavenly aroma. They can be bought dried from online sources. Left to soak overnight, they will perfume your kitchen with a fragrance of autumn woods and damp earth.

braised beef with mushrooms

1 cup (5 oz/155 g) unbleached all-purpose flour

Fine sea salt and freshly ground black pepper

2 lb (1 kg) beef rump roast, chuck roast, or skirt steak, cut into slices ½ inch (12 mm) thick

⅓ cup (80 ml) olive oil

2 sprigs *each* fresh thyme, oregano, and marjoram or 1 teaspoon *each* dried thyme, oregano, and marjoram

1 sprig fresh rosemary or ½ teaspoon dried rosemary

2 yellow onions, thinly sliced

2 tomatoes, cored

3 cloves garlic, crushed

1 cup (250 ml) white wine

1 bay leaf

2 pinches freshly grated nutmeg

1 oz (30 g) bittersweet chocolate

2 oz (60 g) dried wild mushrooms, soaked overnight in water to cover

3 cups (24 fl oz/750 ml) beef stock, preferably homemade (page 179)

serves 6

Put the flour in a shallow bowl and season with salt and pepper. Lightly dredge the beef slices on both sides, shaking off any excess flour.

In a heavy Dutch oven or a flameproof ceramic baking dish with a lid, heat the olive oil over medium heat. Working in batches as necessary, add the beef and brown on all sides, about 5 minutes. Using tongs, transfer the beef to a plate. Reserve the pot with the remaining oil.

Next, make a *sofregit*. If using fresh herb sprigs, tie them in a bundle with kitchen string and set aside. Return the pot to medium heat, add the onions, and sauté until soft, 5–7 minutes. Cut the tomatoes in half crosswise and, using a handheld grater, grate the pulp into the pot. Discard the skins. Add the garlic and cook, stirring occasionally, for about 4 minutes. Add the wine, the herb bundle or dried herbs, the bay leaf, and the nutmeg. Then grate the chocolate into the pot. Simmer over medium heat until the ingredients begin to form a sauce, about 5 minutes.

Drain the mushrooms in a sieve lined with cheesecloth, reserving the liquid, and add the mushrooms to the pot. Return the beef to the pot, along with any accumulated juices. Add the stock and enough of the mushroom-soaking liquid to cover the beef. Season to taste with salt and pepper.

Bring to a simmer, reduce the heat to low, cover partially, and cook until the beef is thoroughly tender and the sauce thick and concentrated, about 1 hour. Remove and discard the herb bundle, if used, and the bay leaf. Transfer to a serving dish or serve directly from the pot.

WINE SUGGESTION: A RICH, BEEFY, TANNIC RED FROM THE MONTSANT OR PRIORAT

The region of Extremadura, home of the *conquistadores*, is a land of wide horizons and sprawling pastures where huge flocks still graze. This robust dish was traditionally cooked up in a black iron pot over a wood fire in the open air. Baby goat being a tougher meat than lamb, the dish benefits from patient simmering.

kid stew

3 lb (1.5 kg) kid (baby goat) meat, on the bone, chopped into 2- to 3-inch (5- to 7.5-cm) pieces (ask your butcher to do this for you)

Fine sea salt and freshly ground black pepper

4 tablespoons (60 ml) olive oil

6 cloves garlic

1 large yellow onion, finely diced

1 red bell pepper, seeded and finely diced

1 teaspoon *pimentón* (Spanish smoked pepper)

2 cups (500 ml) *vino de pitarra,* fino sherry, or other strong, dry white wine

1 slice brown bread, crust removed

2 bay leaves, central vein removed, torn into small pieces

serves 6

In a large glass or ceramic bowl, season the kid meat generously with salt and pepper.

In a heavy cast-iron casserole dish with a lid or a Dutch oven, heat 3 tablespoons of the olive oil over medium heat. Add the garlic and fry until golden. Using a slotted spoon, transfer to a small bowl and set aside.

Add the kid pieces to the pot and cook over medium heat until evenly browned. Do not hurry this process; it may take 15 minutes or longer. Using tongs, transfer the meat to a platter and set aside.

Add the onion and bell pepper to the pot and sauté until soft and lightly browned, 5–7 minutes. Sprinkle in the *pimentón* and cook, stirring, for 30 seconds. Pour in half of the wine and stir to scrape up any browned bits from the pan bottom. Simmer for 1 minute to burn off the alcohol.

In a small frying pan, heat the remaining 1 tablespoon olive oil over medium-high heat. Add the brown bread slice and fry, turning once, until crispy on both sides. Transfer to paper towels to drain.

In a mortar and pestle, combine the garlic cloves, the fried bread, and the bay leaves and pound to a moist, crumbly paste.

Return the meat to the pot and stir into the onion mixture.

Add the remaining wine to the mortar and stir to dilute. Spoon into the pot and mix well to combine with the meat and vegetables.

Bring to a boil, cover, reduce the heat to very low, and cook gently for 2–3 hours, stirring occasionally and adding a little water if needed. The meat should be completely tender and coated in a thick sauce. Serve directly from the pot.

COOK'S NOTE: This dish improves by being served the next day. Accompany with oven-fried potatoes.

WINE SUGGESTION: A BLACKCURRANTY, HERBACEOUS RED FROM EXTREMADURA

sides

The blame for boiled cauliflower's bad reputation partly lies with careless cooks, who allow it to become watery and insipid. Looking for a way to give back some respect to this humble dish, I hit upon the idea of serving it whole, dressed with a zingy herb *vinagreta*, as a worthy partner for barbecued chorizo sausages.

steamed whole cauliflower with herb dressing

Fine sea salt

1 whole head of cauliflower (about 2 lb/1 kg), trimmed

FOR THE DRESSING

1 teaspoon Dijon mustard

1 tablespoon runny honey

¼ cup (60 ml) white wine vinegar

Fine sea salt and freshly ground black pepper

A few leaves/sprigs *each* of the following fresh herbs, minced: basil, chives, cilantro, parsley, and summer savory

½ cup (125 ml) extra-virgin olive oil

serves 4

In a large pot, bring 2 inches (5 cm) of salted water to a boil.

Place the whole cauliflower in the pan, cover tightly, and reduce the heat to very low and simmer gently until al dente, 5–6 minutes. Test the cauliflower stem with the point of a sharp knife—it should not be entirely soft.

Carefully lift out the cauliflower, drain thoroughly, and place on a round serving platter.

To make the dressing, in a small bowl, whisk together the mustard, honey, and vinegar. Season well with salt and pepper. Add the herbs and olive oil and whisk well. Drizzle the dressing over the cauliflower and serve at once.

WINE SUGGESTION: A FRESH, APPLE-FRUITY WHITE MADE FROM THE VERDEJO GRAPE (D.O. RUEDA)

The combination of sweet, juicy raisins and aromatic pine nuts, a culinary heritage dating back to medieval times, is usually associated with spinach but works even better with Swiss chard, whose juicy richness benefits from the lift of sweet and nutty flavors. This makes a great side dish for oven-roasted meats.

swiss chard with raisins & pine nuts

¼ cup (1½ oz/45 g) raisins, preferably golden

3 tablespoons extra-virgin olive oil

3 tablespoons pine nuts

1¾ lb (875 g) Swiss chard

2 cloves garlic, each cut lengthwise into 4 slices

2 oz (60 g) serrano ham, finely chopped

Fine sea salt and freshly ground black pepper

serves 4

In a small bowl, cover the raisins with warm water and soak until plump, about 15 minutes. Drain and set aside.

In a frying pan over medium heat, heat 1 tablespoon of the olive oil. Add the pine nuts and cook, lifting and swirling the pan often, until the nuts are just golden, about 2 minutes. Pour onto a plate to cool.

Trim off the chard stems. Selecting the most tender stems, cut them into ½-inch (12-mm) pieces and set aside. Cut alongside and remove the tough center veins from the leaves. Cut the leaves crosswise into 1-inch (2.5-cm) strips. Rinse the leaves and shake, leaving some water clinging to them. Place in a bowl and set aside.

In a sauté pan over medium-high heat, heat the remaining 2 tablespoons olive oil. Add the garlic and cook, stirring occasionally, until golden on both sides, 2–3 minutes. Remove and discard the garlic.

Add the chard stems and ham to the sauté pan and cook, stirring, until the ham is golden, about 1 minute. Mix in the chard leaves, pressing to pack them down. Cover the pan for 1 minute. Using tongs, turn the chard so the unwilted leaves are moved to the bottom of the pan. Cover and cook for 1 minute longer. Repeat until all of the chard leaves are wilted. Add the raisins and pine nuts and cook uncovered, stirring often, until most of the liquid has evaporated and the chard is as tender as desired, 3–5 minutes longer. Season to taste with salt and pepper.

Transfer to a warmed serving dish and serve at once.

PAIRING SUGGESTION: AN ARTISANAL BEER—PERHAPS A DARK, FULL-BODIED STOUT OR PORTER

When the first baby fava beans come into season in early spring, Spanish cooks pounce on them. When the beans are fresh and tiny, before the skins turn leathery, they are one of the most delectable foods in the world. This is a thoroughly traditional dish, but one that seems modern at the same time.

catalan-style fava beans

Fine sea salt and freshly ground black pepper

6 cups (2 lb/1 kg) shelled fava beans, preferably young, tender beans

½ cup (125 ml) olive oil

6 slices pancetta or unsmoked bacon, cut into 2-inch (5-cm) lengths

2 small true spring onions or green onions, white and pale green parts, finely chopped

4 cloves garlic, minced

1 cup (250 ml) dry white wine, or as needed

6 sprigs fresh flat-leaf parsley, 1 bay leaf, and 3 fresh mint sprigs, tied into a bundle with kitchen string

Shredded fresh mint leaves for garnish

Warm crusty bread for serving

serves 6

Unless you are using very small, young fava beans, you will need to remove their tough inner skins. Bring a pot of water to a boil. Salt the water and add the fava beans. Blanch for 1–2 minutes, then drain and rinse under cold running water. Pinch each bean and squeeze to pop the bean free of its skin. Set the skinned beans aside.

In a heavy frying pan over medium heat, heat the olive oil. Add the pancetta and fry until golden, about 5 minutes. Using a slotted spoon, transfer to paper towels to drain.

Add the onions to the same pan and sauté until softened, about 4 minutes. Add the garlic and sauté for about 2 minutes longer. Add the fava beans, stir, and pour in the wine. Season with salt and pepper, add the herb bundle, and stir to combine. Place the pancetta on top of the beans. Cover, reduce the heat to low, and simmer, shaking the pan occasionally and adding more wine if the mixture dries out, until the beans are tender, 10–15 minutes.

Uncover and mix together with a spoon. Let simmer for 1–2 minutes longer.

Stir the shredded mint leaves into the beans. Remove and discard the herb bundle, transfer the beans to a serving dish, and serve with the bread.

WINE SUGGESTION: A WHITE RIOJA FROM THE VIURA GRAPE

The artichoke is perhaps Spain's best-loved vegetable. When the first spiky globes appear in the markets, in February or March, Spanish cooks buy them by the bagful to prepare in a dozen ways, from fried to chargrilled and even raw. This simple stew is, however, my favorite way with artichokes. Use the small, tight, pale green ones if you can find them.

artichokes with almond sauce

Dash of vinegar

5 lb (2.5 kg) whole small artichokes

5 tablespoons (80 ml) olive oil

1 yellow onion, finely chopped

4 oz (125 g) serrano ham, diced

2 cloves garlic, minced

Juice of 1 lemon

1 cup (250 ml) dry white wine

2 cups (16 fl oz/500 ml) chicken or vegetable stock, preferably homemade (page 178)

Fine sea salt and freshly ground black pepper

1 slice country bread, crust removed, plus more for serving

6 tablespoons (2 oz/60 g) raw blanched almonds, ground

serves 4

Fill a large bowl with cold water and add a dash of vinegar.

To prepare the artichokes, cut off the stem up to 2 inches (5 cm) from the base, slice off the top part of the artichoke, and tear off the hard outer leaves. Halve each lengthwise and, with a small sharp knife, remove the hairs of the "choke" unless they are very fine. Plunge into the acidulated water until needed (the vinegar prevents discoloring and oxidation).

In a heavy casserole dish with a lid, heat 3 tablespoons of the olive oil over medium-high heat. Add the onion and ham and sauté until the onion is just beginning to color, about 5 minutes. Add the garlic and cook, stirring occasionally, for a further minute.

Drain the artichokes and add to the pot, stirring to combine with the onion mixture. Pour in the lemon juice and wine, bring back to a boil, and simmer until the alcohol has evaporated, about 2 minutes. Add the stock, stir well, and season with salt and pepper. Cover tightly, reduce the heat to very low, and simmer gently until the artichokes are just tender, 20–25 minutes.

In a small saucepan, heat the remaining 2 tablespoons olive oil over medium-high heat. Add the bread slice and fry until golden brown on both sides. Transfer to a mortar and pestle, add the almonds, and mash together to an even paste. Stir this mixture into the artichokes and simmer gently until the sauce has thickened slightly, 5–10 minutes.

Remove from the heat and let cool a little before serving with plenty of country bread to mop up the juices.

WINE SUGGESTION: A CRISP, CITRUS-FRESH WHITE RUEDA, WITH THE BITTER TWIST TYPICAL OF THE VERDEJO GRAPE

The Spanish love of eggplant owes much to the Moorish influx of the early Middle Ages. Shreds of that culture still remain in twenty-first-century Spain—like this Andalucían dish from the fabled city of Córdoba.

fried eggplant with honey

2 cups (500 ml) ice-cold lager beer

2 lb (1 kg) eggplant, cut into strips 1 inch (2.5 cm) thick

FOR THE BATTER

½ cup (2½ oz/75 g) unbleached all-purpose flour

1 teaspoon baking powder

Fine sea salt

½ cup (125 ml) ice-cold lager beer

1 large egg white

1 teaspoon fine sea salt

Oil for frying (olive oil or a mixture of olive and sunflower oils)

2 tablespoons *miel de caña* (see Cook's Note) or runny honey

serves 6

In a deep bowl, pour the beer over the eggplant strips. Let stand, turning occasionally, for 30–60 minutes.

Meanwhile, make the batter. In a bowl, combine the flour, baking powder, and a generous pinch of salt. Add the beer in a thin stream, mixing with a fork until the batter has the consistency of light cream.

In a large bowl, whisk the egg white until stiff peaks form, then fold into the batter. Cover and leave in the fridge until needed (at least 30 minutes), stirring again just before using.

Drain the eggplant strips and pat them dry. Sprinkle them with the 1 teaspoon salt.

Pour oil into a deep, heavy frying pan or deep fryer to a depth of 2 inches (5 cm) and heat over medium-high heat. Working in batches of 3 or 4, coat the eggplant strips in the batter and fry, turning with a skimmer until deep golden brown on all sides. Drain on paper towels and transfer to a warmed serving platter.

Drizzle with the *miel de caña* and serve at once.

COOK'S NOTE: Use the Spanish sugar cane syrup *miel de caña* if you can find it; otherwise, a runny bee honey will do fine. Hot tip: the eggplants' initial soaking in cold beer helps prevent oiliness.

WINE SUGGESTION: A GLASS OF RICHLY HONEYED YET DRY OLOROSO SHERRY

Olive oil, vinegar, and pounded hard-boiled egg: simplicity itself. This very Spanish take on vinaigrette is child's play to make, and it turns out to be a winner. It's perfect as a dip for crunchy crudités—try it with batons of fennel or zucchini—but the new season's asparagus is the best vehicle of all.

asparagus with egg vinaigrette

Fine sea salt and freshly ground black pepper

1¼ lb (675 g) green asparagus, tough ends trimmed

2 hard-boiled large eggs, peeled and chopped

5 tablespoons (80 ml) extra-virgin olive oil

2 tablespoons sherry vinegar

6 sprigs fresh flat-leaf parsley, leaves minced

serves 4

In a saucepan, bring a few inches of salted water to a boil. Place a colander over the pan and steam the asparagus (covering the spears and the colander with a lid) until just tender, about 5 minutes. (Alternatively, use an asparagus steamer.)

In a mortar and pestle, combine the hard-boiled eggs, olive oil, vinegar, parsley, ½ teaspoon salt, and pepper to taste. Stir with the pestle just to form a dressing.

Serve the asparagus on a platter with the dressing in a separate bowl for guests to help themselves.

WINE SUGGESTION: ASPARAGUS IS NOTORIOUSLY DIFFICULT TO MATCH WITH WINE, BUT A FINO SHERRY LIKE TIO PEPE WORKS WELL

Autumn's wild mushroom harvest begins to arrive in Catalunya's greenmarkets from forests and mountains at the beginning of October, after the first rains, and are eagerly snapped up. One of the best uses for this delicacy is also the simplest: oven roasted with a *picada*, the mixture of herbs, bread crumbs, and spices often added to Catalan dishes.

oven-roasted wild mushrooms with garlic & parsley

1 lb (500 g) fresh mixed wild mushrooms, wiped clean

½ cup (125 ml) olive oil

Fine sea salt and freshly ground black pepper

FOR THE PICADA

2 cloves garlic, quartered

Fine sea salt

Handful of fresh flat-leaf parsley leaves, roughly chopped

1 tablespoon extra-virgin olive oil

⅓ cup (½ oz/15 g) fresh bread crumbs

Butter for greasing

serves 4

Preheat the oven to 400°F (200°C) and set a rack in the upper third of the oven. Cut any large mushrooms in half lengthwise or into pieces, leaving the smaller mushrooms whole. In a large, dry frying pan, sweat the mushrooms over low heat to remove any excess moisture, about 5 minutes. Add the olive oil and season with salt and pepper. Raise the heat to medium-high and sauté, turning the mushrooms to coat all sides, for about 5 minutes. Remove from the heat and set aside.

To make the *picada,* using a mortar and pestle, crush together the garlic and ½ teaspoon salt, then add the parsley and olive oil and grind until a thick, smooth paste forms. Add the bread crumbs and mix well.

Butter a roasting pan in which the mushrooms will fit in a single layer. Transfer the mushrooms to the pan and drizzle the *picada* over them. Roast on the top rack until the mushrooms are sizzling, about 5 minutes. Turn on the broiler and broil until lightly browned, 1–2 minutes longer. Transfer to a warmed platter and serve at once.

WINE SUGGESTION: A DENSELY FLAVORED, POWERFUL RED WINE FROM D.O. TORO

Here is proof, if any were needed, that the best Spanish dishes often come in the plainer packages. And what could be plainer than boiled vegetables dressed with olive oil and lemon? The *hervido* is a perfect choice when you feel like something virtuous and nourishing, perhaps on a cold winter's day after a long walk.

simmered vegetables with olive oil & lemon

Coarse sea salt

4 lb (1.8 kg) vegetables, such as potato, leek, onion, winter squash, broccoli, carrot, turnip, celery root, and/or green beans (see Cook's Note)

2 lemons, cut into wedges

1 cup (250 ml) extra-virgin olive oil

2 tablespoons Maldon or other top-quality flaky sea salt

serves 6

Bring a large pot of water to a boil. Throw in 1 teaspoon coarse sea salt.

Peel the vegetables if necessary and chop into large pieces.

Reduce the heat and add the vegetables to simmer, starting with the dense or root vegetables (winter squash, carrot, turnip) and finishing with the ones that need less cooking (broccoli, green beans, etc). Cook until tender.

Drain the vegetables, reserving the broth, and arrange on a serving platter.

Serve the lemon wedges, olive oil, and Maldon salt in 3 small bowls. Offer each guest a selection of the vegetables plus a little broth, and pass the condiments around. (The broth can also be ladled into mugs and drunk, if you like.)

COOK'S NOTE: Root vegetables and other winter crops are best for this dish. Bell peppers, eggplant, zucchini, and other summer vegetables are not suitable. Apart from the lemon and olive oil, I like to serve a bowl of hot sauce on the side.

WINE SUGGESTION: AN UNCOMPLICATED, EASY-DRINKING RED FROM RIOJA

This dish from southern Navarra is made in spring and early summer using the peerless produce of the vegetable plots along the banks of the Ebro river. Use the freshest seasonal vegetables you can find. The basic elements are given here, but green beans, asparagus, even spinach and zucchini are also welcome to the party.

vegetable menestra

Fine sea salt and freshly ground black pepper

1 lb (500 g) shelled, blanched, and peeled fava beans (from about 3 lb/1.5 kg in the pod)

¾ lb (375 g) slender young carrots, trimmed and chopped into 1½-inch (4-cm) lengths

1 lemon

6 small or medium artichokes

¼ cup (60 ml) olive oil

4 green onions, including pale green parts, chopped

2 or 3 cloves garlic, minced

8 oz (250 g) serrano ham, diced

1 tablespoon flour

3 tablespoons tomato sauce

6 tablespoons (90 ml) vegetable or chicken stock preferably homemade (page 178)

2 lb (1 kg) English peas, shelled (about 10 oz/ 315 g shelled peas)

Chopped fresh flat-leaf parsley or mint for garnish

serves 4

Fill a saucepan with salted water and bring to a boil. Add the shelled fava beans and boil until tender but still firm, 5–10 minutes, depending upon their size. Drain and set aside.

Refill the same saucepan with salted water and bring to a boil. Add the carrots and boil until tender but still firm, 5–7 minutes. Drain and set aside.

Fill a large bowl with cold water. Cut the lemon in half and squeeze the juice into the water. Working with 1 artichoke, remove all the leaves until you reach the pale green heart. Pare away the dark green area from the base. Cut the artichoke into quarters lengthwise and scoop out and discard the choke from each piece. Drop into the lemon water to prevent discoloration. When all the artichokes are trimmed, drain and place in a saucepan with salted water to cover. Bring to a boil and cook until tender, 15–20 minutes; the timing depends upon the size of the artichokes. Drain and set aside.

In a large frying pan, heat the olive oil over medium heat. Add the green onions and garlic and sauté very briefly. Add the ham and sauté for 1–2 minutes. Add the favas, carrots, and artichokes and swirl them in the oil for 1–2 minutes. Sprinkle with the flour, salt, and pepper, then stir in the tomato sauce and stock. Add the peas and bring to a simmer. Reduce the heat to medium-low and cook until the pan juices are thickened, about 10 minutes.

Taste and adjust the seasoning. Transfer to a platter, garnish with parsley, and serve.

WINE SUGGESTION: AN ELEGANT, FULL-FLAVORED CHARDONNAY FROM NAVARRA

Closely related to other famous cabbage-and-potato combinations like the English "bubble and squeak" and the Irish colcannon, *trinxat* (meaning "chopped" or "shredded") is a staple of the Catalan Pyrenees and Andorra. This comforting winter dish calls for a deep green, well-flavored cabbage variety like Savoy.

cabbage & potato trinxat

3 tablespoons olive oil

2 medium all-purpose potatoes, diced

1 leek, white and pale green parts, diced

½ large cabbage, cored and finely chopped

6 oz (170 g) pancetta or bacon, thinly sliced, plus 6 thin strips pancetta or smoked bacon for garnish

3 cloves garlic, thinly sliced

Fine sea salt and freshly ground black pepper

Fresh thyme leaves for garnish

serves 6

In a deep, heavy sauté pan, heat the olive oil over medium-high heat. Add the potatoes and leek and sauté until lightly browned. Add the cabbage, mix well, and add just enough water to cover the vegetables. Cover and simmer until the potatoes are tender, 20 minutes. Drain and set aside.

Dry the pan, add the sliced pancetta, and place over medium heat. Gently fry for a few minutes until it has released some of its fat, then add the garlic and fry until it is just beginning to color. Add the potato and cabbage mixture and season with a little salt and plenty of pepper. Reduce the heat to low and cook, using a skimmer to break up the potatoes a little and turn the mixture as it begins to brown, about 10 minutes. Remove from the heat and adjust the seasoning.

In a small frying pan, fry the pancetta strips over medium heat until crispy.

Turn the potato mixture out onto a serving platter, forming it into a rough patty shape, and place the fried pancetta strips on top. Alternatively, use a tubular, bottomless mold to make 6 equal cylinders of *trinxat,* and serve each with a crispy pancetta strip. Garnish with fresh thyme leaves.

COOK'S NOTE: Serve with Dijon mustard, country bread, and a bowl of radishes or other crunchy salad item.

WINE SUGGESTION: PAIR WITH A HEARTY, TANNIC RED FROM A PYRENEAN D.O. SUCH AS EMPORDÀ OR SOMONTANO

Tumbet, a hearty all-vegetable bake, has been a firm fixture of my summer cookery repertoire ever since, on a trip to Mallorca many years ago, I watched my friend Mari Creu make the dish at her house in the Tramuntana mountains. Mari Creu taught me the importance of frying and draining each vegetable separately.

mallorcan vegetable bake

Fine sea salt and freshly ground black pepper

2 medium eggplants, cut into ½-inch (12-mm) slices

2 cups (500 ml) olive oil

2 large all-purpose potatoes, cut into ½-inch (12-mm) slices

2 red bell peppers and 2 green bell peppers, seeded and broken into 1-inch (2.5-cm) pieces

6 large ripe tomatoes, peeled, seeded, and finely chopped (or grated; see Cook's Note)

1 sprig fresh marjoram, leaves minced

2 cloves garlic, minced

serves 6

In a glass bowl, lightly salt the eggplant slices, cover with a dry kitchen towel, and let stand for 1 hour. Rinse well and pat dry.

In a wide, shallow frying pan, heat the oil over medium-high heat. Add the potato slices and fry on both sides until just beginning to brown. Using a slotted spoon, transfer to paper towels to drain, then place in a terra-cotta baking dish in a single layer.

Next, fry the eggplant slices on both sides until just golden brown, draining on paper towels and then placing in a layer on top of the potatoes. Lastly, fry the bell peppers, drain, and add them in a third layer.

Preheat the oven to 350°F (180°C).

In a saucepan, combine the chopped tomatoes with the marjoram and garlic and gently heat until the mixture forms a thick sauce, 8–10 minutes. Season with salt and pepper. Pour the sauce evenly over the vegetable layers and bake in the oven until the top is bubbling and lightly browned, 25–30 minutes.

Let cool and serve the *tumbet* warm or at room temperature.

COOK'S NOTE: Instead of peeling and chopping, a common Spanish way with tomatoes is to slice them in half crosswise and rub the cut side against a handheld grater. (This works only if the tomatoes are really ripe.)

WINE SUGGESTION: A MALLORCAN RED MADE FROM LOCAL GRAPES CALLET AND MANTO NEGRO

In high summer, glossy purple-black eggplants crowd the market stalls, and Spaniards are happy to eat them every which way, from fried and baked to pickled and stewed. This recipe for eggplants with a rich meat stuffing comes originally from the Balearic Islands.

stuffed eggplants

3 long eggplants, such as Italian or Asian, about 6 oz (170 g) each

Fine sea salt and freshly ground black pepper

1 tablespoon plus ¼ cup (60 ml) olive oil

1 yellow onion, finely chopped

6 cloves garlic, minced

8 oz (250 g) ground pork

8 oz (250 g) ground veal

4 large ripe tomatoes, peeled, seeded, and minced

2 fresh marjoram or oregano sprigs

1 bay leaf

½ cup (125 ml) half-and-half

3 oz (90 g) Mahón, Parmigiano-Reggiano, or other hard cow's milk cheese, freshly grated

Handful of fresh flat-leaf parsley leaves, minced

serves 6

Cut the eggplants in half lengthwise. Scoop out the flesh into a colander, leaving a shell with walls about ½ inch (12 mm) thick. Sprinkle the shells and flesh with salt. Place the shells cut side down on paper towels and let the eggplant drain for about 1 hour. (This salting draws out bitter juices.) Rinse in cold water and dry thoroughly.

Preheat the oven to 350°F (180°C). Select a shallow ovenproof dish in which the eggplant shells will fit, cut side up, snugly side by side. (This will help them to retain their shape while cooking.) Rub the shells all over with the 1 tablespoon olive oil. Arrange in the dish and bake until soft, 15–20 minutes.

Meanwhile, finely chop the eggplant flesh. In a heavy frying pan, heat the ¼ cup (60 ml) olive oil over medium heat. Add the onion and sauté until softened, about 6 minutes. Then add the garlic, chopped eggplant, pork, and veal. Cook, stirring often, until the meat is nicely browned, about 10 minutes. Add the tomatoes, marjoram, and bay leaf and season to taste with salt and pepper. Continue to cook, stirring, until the liquid has almost entirely evaporated, about 10 minutes longer. Discard the bay leaf.

Spoon the filling into the eggplant shells. Drizzle a little half-and-half over each one and top with the cheese and parsley. If desired, sprinkle with pepper. Bake until the cheese is bubbling and golden brown, 25–30 minutes. Let cool slightly before serving.

WINE SUGGESTION: A FULL-BODIED, WELL-BALANCED RED FROM THE RIBERA DEL DUERO

Potatoes are a staple of the Spanish diet and are grown throughout the country. This tasty Castilian dish, originally hailing from the province of Palencia, is "important" enough to be a meal in itself.

patatas a la importancia

Olive oil for deep-frying

3 large eggs

About 1½ cups (7½ oz/ 235 g) unbleached all-purpose flour

4 large russet potatoes, about 2 lb (1 kg) total weight, peeled and cut into slices ½ inch (12 mm) thick

1 large yellow onion, finely chopped

5 cloves garlic, minced

2 cups (12 oz/375 g) peeled, seeded, and chopped tomato (fresh or canned)

Pinch of sugar (optional)

2 cups (16 fl oz/500 ml) beef stock, preferably homemade (page 179)

Fine sea salt and freshly ground black pepper

serves 4–6

Pour olive oil into a wide, deep frying pan to a depth of 2 inches (5 cm) and heat over medium-high heat to 350°F (180°C) on a deep-frying thermometer. Meanwhile, in a shallow bowl, whisk the eggs until blended. Spread the flour on a plate.

When the oil is ready, working in batches, coat the potato slices in the beaten eggs and then dredge in the flour, shaking off any excess. Slip them into the hot oil and fry until golden, 3–5 minutes. Using a slotted spoon, transfer to a flameproof casserole dish or large frying pan and set aside.

Drain off all but about 2 tablespoons of the oil from the frying pan and place over medium heat. Add the onion and garlic and sauté until tender, about 10 minutes. Add the tomatoes and simmer until slightly thickened, about 5 minutes. If the tomatoes taste tart, add the sugar. Stir in 1 tablespoon flour, then pour the mixture over the potatoes.

Pour the stock over the potatoes and season with salt and pepper. Bring to a simmer, then reduce the heat to low and cook, uncovered, until tender, about 35 minutes. Serve hot directly from the dish or pan.

WINE SUGGESTION: A RED WINE FROM THE D.O. VINOS DE LA TIERRA DE CASTILLA Y LEÓN

On a cold winter's day in the vineyards of La Rioja, a rich aroma wafts among the vines. The workers have taken a break from their pruning to enjoy a warming plateful of *patatas a la riojana*, the local dish of potatoes with chorizo, which is traditionally cooked in an iron pot over an open fire. (Riojano gourmets insist that the potatoes should be roughly broken with the hands, not cut with a knife, in order to better release their starch.)

la rioja–style potatoes

¼ cup (60 ml) olive oil, or as needed

4 large new potatoes, about 2 lb (1 kg) total weight, peeled and cut into 1½-inch (4-cm) chunks

8 oz (250 g) Spanish-style semicured chorizo sausage

1 yellow onion, chopped

1 red bell or piquillo pepper, seeded and chopped

2–4 cloves garlic, minced

2 teaspoons *pimentón dulce* (sweet Spanish smoked pepper)

1 small fresh red chile, seeded and minced

Fine sea salt and freshly ground black pepper

2 tablespoons chopped fresh flat-leaf parsley

serves 8

In a large frying pan, heat the olive oil over medium heat. Add the potatoes and sauté, stirring often, until pale gold, 10–15 minutes. Using a slotted spoon, transfer to a bowl. Add the chorizo to the pan and fry, turning as needed, until crisp and golden, about 4 minutes, adding more oil if needed. Using tongs, transfer the chorizo to a cutting board. When cool enough to handle, cut into ½-inch (12-mm) pieces.

Add the onion to the pan and sauté over medium heat, stirring occasionally, until golden, about 15 minutes. Add the bell pepper, garlic, *pimentón,* and chile and sauté until the onion has absorbed all the spices, about 5 minutes longer.

Return the potatoes and chorizo to the pan and pour in 1 cup (250 ml) water. Bring to a simmer, reduce the heat to low, cover tightly, and simmer until the potatoes are tender, about 15 minutes. Season with salt and pepper. Transfer to a serving dish, sprinkle with the parsley, and serve warm.

WINE SUGGESTION: WHAT ELSE?—A FULL-BODIED CRIANZA (OAKED RED) FROM RIOJA

The empanada, a sort of flat double-crusted pie, is a much-loved staple found in every street-corner bakery in the northwestern Spanish region of Galicia. Most commonly featuring a filling of tuna and peppers, ground meat, or shellfish, this vegetable-based (but not vegetarian) version combines juicy Swiss chard with the empanada's most essential basic ingredient: a base of sweet, soft slow-cooked onion.

empanada with swiss chard & chorizo

FOR THE DOUGH

1 heaping teaspoon active dry yeast

½ cup (125 ml) warm water

Pinch of sugar

3 cups (15 oz/450 g) bread flour, or as needed

2 large eggs, beaten

½ cup (125 ml) white wine

1 scant teaspoon table salt

1 tablespoon butter, diced, at room temperature

FOR THE FILLING

1 lb (500 g) Swiss chard (about 6 stalks)

Fine sea salt and freshly ground black pepper

¼ cup (60 ml) olive oil

3 yellow onions, coarsely chopped

1 bay leaf

3 cloves garlic, minced

4 oz (125 g) Spanish-style semicured chorizo sausage, skinned and finely diced

2 hard-boiled large eggs, peeled and chopped

To make the dough, in a small bowl, combine the yeast, warm water, and sugar, mixing well. Cover and let stand in a warm place until the mixture begins to bubble.

Put the flour in a large, heavy bowl and make a small well in the flour. Add the yeast mixture, incorporating the flour with a fork, then add the 2 beaten eggs, wine, and salt, continuing to mix first with the fork and then with your hands, until a soft, pliant dough forms. Add the butter and knead for 5 minutes, adding a little flour if the dough seems sticky. Cover and let rise in a warm place until doubled in volume, 1–2 hours.

To make the filling, separate the chard's wide stalks from the leaves. Chop the stalks into 1-inch (2.5-cm) pieces and roughly chop the leaves. In a sauté pan, bring a small amount of salted water to a simmer over medium-high heat. Add the chard stems and simmer the stalks for 5 minutes, then add the leaves, cover, and simmer until wilted, 5 minutes more. Drain thoroughly through a sieve, pressing out excess water. Set aside.

In a heavy frying pan, heat the olive oil over low heat. Add the onions and bay leaf and gently stew, stirring frequently, until soft and pale yellow. Do not hurry this process; it may take 15 minutes or longer. Add the garlic and chorizo and cook for 5 minutes more. Finally, add the drained chard to the onion mixture and cook, stirring well, until the filling is silky but not sloppy and most of the vegetable juices have evaporated. Add the hard-boiled eggs and season well with salt and pepper. Let cool slightly.

Olive oil for greasing

1 large egg, beaten, for brushing

serves 8

Preheat the oven to 350°F (180°C) and grease a baking sheet with olive oil.

Divide the dough into 2 pieces, one a little larger than the other. On a floured surface, roll out the larger piece into a 12-by-14-inch (30-by-35-cm) rectangle. Using the rolling pin if necessary, transfer the pastry to the baking sheet. Spoon the filling onto the pastry, leaving a 2-inch (5-cm) border around the edge. Roll out the other piece of dough to form a smaller rectangle and place on top of the filling, using your fingers to roughly crimp and seal the edges of the pie.

Brush the top of the pie with beaten egg. Make half a dozen slashes across the surface of the pie with a sharp knife. Bake until the pie is golden yellow on top, 45 minutes.

COOK'S NOTE: The empanada is best eaten warm or at room temperature—never straight from the oven. It makes for a perfect picnic dish.

PAIRING SUGGESTION: A COLD ESTRELLA GALICIA BEER OR WHITE RIBEIRO WINE

sweets

High summer in Spain is the season of the watermelon. The big red-and-green ball becomes the go-to fruit for munching on the beach or in the park, or for finishing off a long lunch in fine style. Nothing is more refreshing on a hot day—except this ridiculously simple water ice, *granizado*, which ramps up the watermelon's chill factor one more notch.

watermelon ice

2 lb (1 kg) watermelon

2½ cups (12 oz/375 g) crushed ice

¼ cup (2 oz/50 g) sugar

Fresh mint leaves for garnish

serves 4

Cut the watermelon into chunks, cutting away the peel and removing the seeds. Place the chunks in the freezer until solid, at least 2 hours.

In a blender, briefly whizz the melon along with the crushed ice and sugar. Serve in glass dishes or glasses, garnished with a mint leaf or two for decoration. The *granizado* can be eaten with either a spoon or a straw (offer both).

WINE SUGGESTION: A PALE FRUITY ROSADO FROM THE ISLAND OF IBIZA

These sweet, eggy fritters, a close relation of French toast, are popular throughout the year in Madrid. But when Holy Week comes round, there is suddenly a whole new excuse to eat them. Oozing with syrup or honey, they are displayed in the windows of renowned *pastelerías* like La Mallorquina and packed up in boxes to be enjoyed at home.

"poor knights" bread fritters

6–8 thick slices day-old coarse country white bread, crusts removed

2 cups (500 ml) milk, or as needed

Orange or lemon zest strips

1 cinnamon stick

Sweet sherry (optional)

3 large eggs

Olive oil for frying

Warmed honey or cinnamon-sugar (see Cook's Note)

serves 6

Cut each bread slice diagonally into 2 triangles. Place in a single layer in a shallow baking pan or baking dish.

Pour the milk into a saucepan over medium heat, add the citrus zest and cinnamon stick, and heat until small bubbles appear along the edges of the pan. Remove from the heat and let steep for about 30 minutes. Remove and discard the cinnamon stick and citrus zest and pour the milk over the bread. If the milk does not cover the bread, add more milk or add sherry as needed. Let stand for 10 minutes so the bread can absorb the milk.

In a shallow bowl, whisk the eggs until blended. Pour olive oil into a large frying pan to a depth of ¼ inch (6 mm) and heat over medium-high heat until hot.

Working in batches, dip the bread into the beaten eggs and place in the hot oil. Fry, turning once, until golden on both sides, 6–8 minutes total. Transfer to individual plates and drizzle with warm honey or sprinkle with cinnamon-sugar. Repeat with the remaining bread, adding more olive oil as needed. Serve at once.

COOK'S NOTE: To make cinnamon-sugar, combine ⅓ cup (2½ oz/60 g) superfine sugar and ½ teaspoon ground cinnamon.

WINE SUGGESTION: A SWEET OLOROSO SHERRY

These dangerously "moreish" almond crisps hail from the market town of Tolosa, outside San Sebastían, where the Gorrotxategui family of confectioners has been making them since 1680. It was from Rafa Gorrotxategui that I learned the technique of bending the cookies into the curved shape which, to Spaniards, recalls that of a terra-cotta roof tile—hence the name *"tejas"* ("tiles").

basque almond cookies

4 cups (1 lb/500 g) ground almonds

2 cups (14 oz/400 g) sugar

1¼ cups (6½ oz/200 g) all-purpose flour

6 large eggs, beaten

Grated zest of ½ lemon

serves 6

Preheat the oven to 350°F (180°C). In a large bowl, stir together the ground almonds, sugar, and flour. Add the beaten eggs and lemon zest and stir well to combine.

Drop teaspoonfuls of the batter onto a nonstick baking sheet, leaving plenty of room for the *tejas* to expand during baking.

Bake until the *tejas* are golden brown on top, about 13 minutes (check them once or twice toward the end of the baking time). Transfer the baking sheet to a wire rack and let cool briefly.

As soon as the *tejas* are cool enough to handle, remove each from the sheet with an icing spatula and drape over a bottle or glass to gently bend into a curved shape. Don't take too long over it, or the *tejas* will harden while still flat.

COOK'S NOTE: These "Tolosa tiles" make a perfect accompaniment for ice creams, zabaglione, or *crema catalana* (page 167)—or serve them on their own at coffee time.

WINE SUGGESTION: A LIGHT, CITRUSY, SWEET MALVASIA FROM THE ISLAND OF MALLORCA

This moist, lightly sweetened sponge cake, known as *tarta de almendras*, combines Spanish citrus with the mild, aromatic Mediterranean flavors of almonds and olive oil. It is delicious served with fruit, and any leftovers make a perfect breakfast or teatime snack.

orange-scented almond torte

⅓ cup (80 ml) olive oil, plus more for greasing

1½ cups (7½ oz/235 g) unbleached all-purpose flour, plus more for dusting

2 teaspoons baking powder

½ teaspoon fine sea salt

½ cup (2½ oz/75 g) coarsely chopped blanched almonds

1 cup (7 oz/200 g) sugar

3 large eggs

1 tablespoon grated orange zest

2 teaspoons vanilla extract

Sliced orange segments or rounds for garnish (optional)

Pomegranate seeds for garnish (optional)

Honey for garnish (optional)

serves 8

Preheat the oven to 350°F (180°C). Grease a 9-inch (23-cm) springform pan, dust it with flour, and shake out the excess.

In a bowl, stir together the flour, baking powder, and salt. In a food processor, combine the almonds and ¼ cup (2 oz/50 g) of the sugar and process until finely ground.

In a bowl, using an electric mixer set on medium-high speed, beat the eggs until frothy. Add the remaining ¾ cup (5 oz/150 g) sugar, raise the speed to high, and beat until thick and pale yellow, 6–8 minutes. Reduce the speed to low and beat in the olive oil, orange zest, and vanilla. Using a rubber spatula, gently fold in the flour and almond mixtures until well blended. Scrape the batter into the prepared pan.

Bake the torte until the top is golden brown and a skewer inserted into the center comes out clean, about 30 minutes. Transfer the pan to a wire rack and let cool for 10 minutes. Run a thin-bladed knife around the edge of the pan to loosen the torte sides, then remove the pan sides. Let cool completely.

Decorate the whole torte or individual slices with orange segments and pomegranate seeds and drizzle with honey, if desired.

WINE SUGGESTION: A VINO NARANJA, A SWEET WINE INFUSED WITH ORANGE PEEL, FROM THE COUNTY OF HUELVA

The region of Aragon is famous for its peaches, and local cooks stop at roadside stalls at the height of the summer to buy basket-fuls of the just-picked, tree-ripened fruit. There are few things I'd rather do with a juicy peach than eat it fresh—but I'm also partial to this simple preparation using sugar, dry red wine, and cinnamon.

peaches in red wine

4 large freestone peaches

2½ cups (625 ml) dry red wine

½ cup (3½ oz/100 g) sugar

Zest of 1 lemon, cut into strips

1 cinnamon stick

⅓ cup (80 ml) good-quality brandy (optional)

serves 4

To peel the peaches, bring a saucepan three-fourths full of water to a boil. Score an X in the blossom end of each peach. Immerse in the boiling water until the skin begins to curl away from the X, about 30 seconds. Using a slotted spoon, transfer to a bowl of cold water, then peel away the skins.

Cut each peach in half through the stem end and remove the pit. Place the peaches in a heatproof bowl.

In a saucepan, combine the wine, sugar, lemon zest, and cinnamon stick over medium heat and bring to a boil, stirring to dissolve the sugar. Add the brandy, if using, then remove from the heat and pour over the peaches. Let cool, then cover and let steep in the wine for 2 days in the refrigerator.

To serve, spoon the peaches, along with some of the liquid, into glass bowls or goblets. Serve cold.

WINE SUGGESTION: A SWEET BUT FRESHLY FRUITY MOSCATEL FROM D.O. MÁLAGA

Although fried custard (literally "fried milk") is popular all over Spain, this version comes from La Mancha. The custard should be firm enough to hold its shape when cut, creamy in texture, and not floury tasting. For an aromatic finish, flambé the *leche frita* with anise liqueur.

leche frita

Clarified unsalted butter or vegetable oil for frying, plus more for greasing

3 cups (750 ml) whole milk

1 lemon zest strip, 2 inches (5 cm) long

1 vanilla bean, split lengthwise

¾ cup (6 oz/170 g) unsalted butter

½ cup (2½ oz/75 g) unbleached all-purpose flour

Pinch of fine sea salt

1 cup (7 oz/200 g) granulated sugar

6 large egg yolks plus 1 or 2 whole large eggs

4–5 cups (1–1¼ lb/500–625 g) fine dried bread crumbs

Confectioners' sugar mixed with ground cinnamon for dusting

serves 8

Grease an 8-by-10-inch (20-by-25-cm) baking pan and place it in the freezer to chill well.

In a saucepan, combine the milk, zest, and vanilla bean and bring to a boil over medium-high heat. Reduce the heat to low, simmer for 10 minutes, then remove from the heat and let steep for 1 hour. Strain the milk, discarding the zest and vanilla bean, and reheat the milk just until small bubbles appear along the edges of the pan. Remove from the heat.

In a separate saucepan, melt the butter over low heat. Add the flour and salt and cook for 5 minutes, stirring constantly to blend well. Gradually whisk in the granulated sugar and the hot milk. Slowly bring to a boil, stirring often and cooking until thickened, about 5 minutes.

Gradually whisk in the egg yolks and continue to stir until the mixture is very thick, 5–7 minutes. Remove from the heat and pour the mixture into the chilled baking pan. Using a rubber spatula, spread to an even thickness of about 1 inch (2.5 cm). Cover and refrigerate until the custard is fully set, at least 2 hours or up to overnight.

When ready to fry, cut the custard into 8 squares or diamonds. In a shallow bowl, beat 1 egg until foamy. (Start with 1 egg and use the second only if needed.) Spread the bread crumbs on a plate.

Pour clarified butter or vegetable oil into a large frying pan to a depth of ½ inch (12 mm) and place over medium heat. When the butter or oil is hot, working in batches, dip the custard pieces into the egg, coating evenly, and then in the bread crumbs, again coating evenly. Fry, turning once, until golden on both sides, 6–8 minutes total. Using a slotted spatula, transfer to paper towels to drain briefly. Keep warm until all the pieces are fried.

Arrange the fried custard pieces on a platter. Dust them with confectioners' sugar mixed with a little cinnamon and serve at once.

WINE SUGGESTION: A LIGHTLY HONEYED LATE-HARVEST MOSCATEL FROM ALICANTE

From Valencian oranges to Canary Island bananas, Aragon peaches, melons from Andalucía, and cherries from Extremadura, Spain is a paradise for fruit. This classic salad is best made in advance, with thoroughly ripe fruit, and left in the fridge for its flavors to meld and mature.

spanish fruit salad

12 large strawberries

Handful *each* cherries, blueberries, and raspberries

½ Galia melon or cantaloupe

1 slice watermelon

2 nectarines

2 peaches

2 kiwifruits

2 Bartlett or Comice pears

2 bananas

Juice of ½ lemon

Juice of 4 Valencia oranges, plus 2 whole oranges

1 grapefruit

2 tablespoons Cointreau (optional)

6 fresh mint leaves

serves 6

Stem and core the strawberries and pit the cherries. In a large glass mixing bowl, combine them with the blueberries and raspberries.

Peel, seed, and chop the melon and watermelon into similar-sized chunks. Leaving the skin on the nectarines, pit and chop them. Peel, pit, and chop the peaches, then peel and chop the kiwifruits. Core and chop the pears. Peel and slice the bananas. Add the chopped and sliced fruit to the bowl. Add the lemon juice and orange juice and mix and toss the fruit well.

Using a sharp knife, peel the oranges and grapefruit, removing both the colorful peel and white pith. Slice alongside each segment to free it from the surrounding membrane, letting the segments and any juice drop into the fruit bowl.

Add the Cointreau, if using, and toss everything again. Cover with plastic wrap and leave in the fridge for at least 1 hour.

Just before serving, roughly tear the mint leaves and mix them in. Serve in individual glass bowls or ramekins, for dessert or breakfast.

WINE SUGGESTION: A FRESH, ORANGEY, SWEET (BUT NOT CLOYING) DESSERT MOSCATEL FROM D.O. MÁLAGA

Turrón, the rich nougat made with almonds, sugar, and egg white, takes a starring role on holiday tables along with the *polvorones*, *mantecados*, and the rest of the universe of Spanish festive sweetmeats. *Turrón* has few roles to play in cuisine, with the honorable exception of this stunning ice cream.

turrón nougat ice cream

1 cup (250 ml) whole milk

2 cups (500 ml) heavy cream

1 cinnamon stick

2 large egg yolks

½ cup (3½ oz/100 g) sugar

1 package (10½ oz/300 g) *turrón de Jijona* or other soft nougat

serves 8

In a saucepan, combine the milk, cream, and cinnamon stick. Place over medium heat and gently heat until just under the boiling point. Remove from the heat and let cool for 5 minutes.

In a bowl, beat together the egg yolks and sugar until the mixture becomes a smooth, pale yellow cream.

Divide the *turrón* into two halves. Chop the first half into ½-inch (12-mm) cubes. Finely dice the second half.

Using a slotted spoon, remove the cinnamon stick from the milk mixture and discard. Add the egg yolk mixture and the cubed *turrón* and stir gently with a wooden spoon until the *turrón* has dissolved. Place over very low heat and cook until the custard is thick enough to coat the back of the spoon. Do not allow it to boil, as the egg yolks will curdle.

Remove from the heat and cover the pan. When completely cool, transfer the custard to a bowl, cover, and place in the fridge for at least 4 hours, and preferably overnight.

Freeze the custard in an ice-cream machine, following the manufacturer's instructions. Just before the end of churning time, tip in the diced *turrón*. Serve right away, or freeze until firm.

COOK'S NOTE: Be sure to choose soft *turrón de Jijona* rather than the brittle Alicante version for this recipe.

WINE SUGGESTION: A RICH, DARK, AGED PEDRO XIMÉNEZ DESSERT WINE (TRY POURING A LITTLE OF THE WINE OVER THE ICE CREAM)

Biscuit de higos, a creamy frozen dessert and an old-school Spanish standard, can be made at any time of year, since it uses dried figs. Its other great advantage is that it doesn't require an ice-cream machine. (Why it's known in Spain as *"biscuit,"* however, remains a mystery!)

fig parfait with walnut & salted caramel sauce

5 oz (155 g) dried figs, stemmed and finely chopped

3 tablespoons good-quality brandy

4 large eggs, separated

1 cup (250 ml) heavy cream

½ cup (3½ oz/100 g) superfine sugar

FOR THE SAUCE

1½ oz (45 g) walnuts

1½ tablespoons unsalted butter

¾ cup (180 ml) light cream

¼ teaspoon fine sea salt

½ cup (3½ oz/100 g) granulated sugar

serves 6

In a small bowl, combine the figs and brandy and let steep for 1 hour, stirring occasionally. Line a 6-inch (15-cm) jelly mold with plastic wrap.

In a large mixing bowl, using a whisk or electric mixer, beat the egg whites until nearly stiff peaks form. Set aside. In another large mixing bowl, using a whisk or electric mixer, whip the cream until just less than firm peaks form. Set aside.

In a small saucepan, heat the superfine sugar and 2 tablespoons water over medium heat, stirring to dissolve the sugar and make a transparent syrup. Remove from the heat and add the egg yolks one by one, stirring all the time to prevent curdling. Add the figs and mix thoroughly.

Fold the fig mixture into the whipped cream, mixing gently with a rubber spatula. Whisk the egg whites again until stiff, then add them to the fig mixture and fold in carefully, making wide sweeping movements with the spatula until the ingredients are well combined. Tip the fig mixture into the prepared mold and freeze for at least 6 hours.

To make the sauce, in a mortar and pestle, pound the walnuts to a thick paste. In a small, heavy saucepan, combine the walnuts, butter, cream, and salt over very low heat. Heat gently, stirring occasionally, until the butter has melted and the mixture is smooth, 3–4 minutes.

Meanwhile, in a heavy saucepan, heat the granulated sugar over high heat, stirring with a wooden spoon, until a thick golden caramel has formed. Do not allow it to burn. Add the walnut mixture to the hot caramel, stirring constantly (be careful: it may spatter on contact). The caramel will solidify into lumps; reduce the heat to very low and stir gently until the lumps have dissolved into the sauce, about 4 minutes. Let cool.

To serve, invert a platter on top of the mold, invert the mold and platter together, and lift off the mold. Remove the plastic wrap. Let rest at room temperature for 5 minutes, then pour the sauce over and serve.

This wobbly milk-and-egg custard with a crown of caramel makes a memorable finish to a Spanish meal. It is normally prepared in individual metal pots known as *flaneras*, specially made for the purpose. These can be difficult to find outside Spain, but you can substitute individual-sized ramekins or small custard cups.

caramel flans

FOR THE CARAMEL

3 tablespoons sugar

2 tablespoons water

FOR THE FLANS

2½ cups (625 ml) whole milk

1 vanilla bean, split lengthwise, or a few drops of vanilla extract

2 whole large eggs plus 6 large egg yolks, at room temperature

1 cup (7 oz/200 g) sugar

Boiling water, as needed

serves 6

To make the caramel, in a small saucepan, combine the sugar and water. Place over medium heat and bring to a boil, then cook without stirring until the mixture becomes a golden brown syrup, about 4 minutes.

Distribute the caramel evenly among six ½-cup (4–fl oz/125-ml) *flaneras*, ramekins, or custard cups, turning each mold to coat it with caramel about halfway up the sides.

To make the flans, in a saucepan, combine the milk and the vanilla bean. Place over low heat and heat until small bubbles appear along the edges of the pan, about 7 minutes. Do not allow the milk to boil.

Place a rack in the center of the oven and preheat to 300°F (150°C).

In a bowl, using a balloon whisk, beat together the eggs, egg yolks, and the sugar until a pale, creamy mousse forms. Add a little of the hot milk, whisking constantly to prevent the yolks from curdling. Add the remaining milk little by little while continuing to whisk. Remove and discard the vanilla bean. Strain the custard through a fine-mesh sieve into the prepared molds, dividing it evenly.

Place the filled molds in a large baking dish and carefully add boiling water to reach halfway up the sides of the molds, creating a water bath.

Bake the flans until they have just set but the centers still jiggle just slightly, 50–60 minutes. To test, touch the surface of the custard lightly with the tip of a knife; it should come away clean. Remove the baking dish from the oven and lift the molds out of the water. Let cool to room temperature, then cover and refrigerate until well chilled, at least 2 hours or up to 6 hours.

To serve, run a sharp, thin knife blade around the inside of each mold, then turn out the custards onto individual plates.

WINE SUGGESTION: A LIGHT, HONEYED DESSERT WINE FROM NAVARRA

Flan is a ubiquitous item on Spanish menus, but this version gives the classic formula a twist. What's interesting is how clearly the flavor of the iconic Spanish sheep's cheese Manchego (probably the country's best known abroad) comes shining through.

manchego cheese flans

FOR THE CARAMEL

3 tablespoons sugar

2 tablespoons water

FOR THE FLANS

3 large eggs, at room temperature

⅓ cup (2½ oz/60 g) sugar

2 cups (500 ml) heavy cream, at room temperature

½ cup (125 ml) whole milk, at room temperature

2 oz (60 g) cured Manchego cheese, grated

serves 4

To make the caramel, in a small saucepan, combine the sugar and water. Place over medium heat and bring to a boil, then cook, without stirring, until the mixture becomes a golden brown syrup, about 4 minutes.

Distribute the caramel evenly among 4 *flaneras,* ramekins, or custard cups, turning each mold to coat it with caramel about halfway up the sides.

Place a rack in the center of the oven and preheat to 400°F (200°C).

To make the flans, in a mixing bowl, using a balloon whisk, beat together the eggs, sugar, cream, and milk until well mixed. Stir in the cheese.

Pour this mixture into the prepared molds and set them in a roasting pan. Add hot tap water to come halfway up the sides of the molds, creating a water bath. Bake the flans until they have just set but the centers still jiggle just slightly, 30–35 minutes. To test, touch the surface of the custard lightly with the tip of a knife; it should come away clean.

Remove the baking dish from the oven and lift the molds out of the water. Let cool to room temperature, then cover and refrigerate until well chilled, at least 2 hours or up to 6 hours.

To serve, run a sharp, thin knife blade around the inside of each mold, and turn out the custards onto individual plates.

WINE SUGGESTION: A LIGHT, HONEYED DESSERT WINE FROM NAVARRA

Crema catalana is made for the springtime feast of St. Joseph, but is also an everyday delicacy prepared in home kitchens throughout Catalunya. The consistency should be neither jellylike nor excessively liquid, just solid enough to be eaten in creamy spoonfuls. To achieve this, stir the custard over very low heat.

crema catalana

8 large egg yolks

¾ cup (5 oz/150 g) sugar

4½ tablespoons (1 oz/30 g) cornstarch

4 cups (1 l) whole milk

Grated zest of ½ lemon

1 cinnamon stick

serves 6

In a bowl, using a balloon whisk, beat together the egg yolks and ½ cup (3½ oz/100 g) of the sugar until pale and creamy, about 6 minutes. Set aside.

In a large bowl, dissolve the cornstarch in ¼ cup (60 ml) of the milk. In a heavy saucepan, combine the remaining 3¾ cups (940 ml) milk, the lemon zest, and the cinnamon stick over low heat and heat until small bubbles form along the edges of the pan, about 10 minutes.

Whisk the egg yolk mixture into the cornstarch mixture until well blended. Add a little of the hot milk, whisking constantly to prevent the yolks from curdling. Add the remaining milk little by little while continuing to whisk.

Strain the mixture through a fine-mesh sieve back into the saucepan used for heating the milk. Place over very low heat and heat slowly, stirring constantly, until the custard is thick enough to coat the back of the spoon, about 15 minutes. Do not let it boil, or the mixture will curdle.

Remove and discard the cinnamon stick. Pour the custard into six 1-cup (250-ml) shallow custard dishes or ramekins or into a 2-qt (2-l) shallow gratin dish and let cool to room temperature. Cover with plastic wrap and refrigerate until well chilled, at least 2 hours or up to 12 hours.

Make the sugar crust no more than 30 minutes before serving, to help it stay crisp. Dust the surface of the cold custards evenly with the remaining ¼ cup (2 oz/50 g) sugar. Using a kitchen torch, and holding it 2–3 inches (5–7.5 cm) from the custard surface, caramelize the sugar by constantly moving the flame over the top until the sugar bubbles. Alternatively, set a rack 3 inches (7.5 cm) below the heat source and turn on the broiler. Place the custard dishes or gratin dish on a baking sheet and broil just until the top is caramelized, about 2 minutes. The burnt sugar should form a thin sheet of golden brown caramel.

WINE SUGGESTION: A SWEET OR SEMISECO (OFF-DRY) SPARKLING CAVA FROM CATALUNYA

Chocolate and olive oil go well together: a popular Spanish playground snack in the old days was bread drizzled with olive oil and sprinkled with chocolate powder. In this unusual version of chocolate mousse, extra-virgin olive oil replaces the typical cream, resulting in a silky texture and an intriguing hint of olive flavor.

chocolate mousse with olive oil

6 oz (170 g) bittersweet chocolate, finely chopped

3 large egg yolks, plus 2 large egg whites

¼ cup (60 ml) extra-virgin olive oil

3 tablespoons warm water

¼ teaspoon fine sea salt

⅛ teaspoon cream of tartar

¼ cup (2 oz/50 g) granulated sugar

½ cup (125 ml) heavy cream

2 teaspoons confectioners' sugar

Chocolate shavings for serving (optional)

serves 4–6

In a heatproof bowl set over, but not touching, a saucepan of barely simmering water, stir the chocolate until melted and smooth. (Alternatively, melt it in a microwave.) Remove from the heat and let cool slightly, then whisk in the egg yolks, olive oil, warm water, and salt until well blended.

In a separate, clean bowl, using an electric mixer set on medium-high speed, beat together the egg whites and the cream of tartar until frothy. Add the granulated sugar and beat until soft peaks form. Fold about one-third of the egg-white mixture into the chocolate mixture until no white streaks remain. Gently fold in the remaining egg-white mixture until well incorporated.

Evenly divide the mousse among 4–6 dessert cups or wineglasses, cover, and refrigerate until well chilled, at least 4 hours or up to overnight.

In a bowl, combine the cream and confectioners' sugar and beat with a balloon whisk until medium-stiff peaks form. Spoon an equal amount of the whipped cream on top of each bowl and sprinkle with chocolate shavings, if you like. Serve at once.

COOK'S NOTE: This recipe includes uncooked egg.

WINE SUGGESTION: A PEDRO XIMÉNEZ SHERRY FROM MONTILLA-MORILES, WITH HINTS OF CHOCOLATE AND DRIED FRUIT

When I lived in Ibiza, I was often surprised at the inventive culinary repertoire of an island little more than 20 miles long and 10 miles wide. A favorite item of mine in local bakeries was this sweet tart made with a filling of eggs and fresh sheep's cheese and its intriguing hint of aniseed in the crust and mint in the filling.

cheese & mint tart

FOR THE PASTRY

1⅔ cups (9 oz/250 g) unbleached all-purpose flour

3 tablespoons granulated sugar

1 teaspoon baking powder

½ teaspoon aniseed

Pinch of fine sea salt

4 tablespoons (2 oz/60 g) cold unsalted butter, diced

Grated zest of 1 lemon

1 large egg, beaten

4 tablespoons anisette, Pernod, or other anise-flavored liqueur

Butter or olive oil for greasing

FOR THE FILLING

14 oz (400 g) fresh sheep's milk cheese (or other fresh cheese)

3 large eggs

1 cup (7 oz/200 g) granulated sugar

12 fresh mint leaves, minced

½ cup (3½ oz/100 g) superfine sugar

Fresh mint leaves for garnish

serves 4–6

To make the pastry, in a large bowl, stir together the flour, granulated sugar, baking powder, aniseed, and salt. Add the butter and rub in with your fingertips until the mixture resembles bread crumbs. (Alternatively, combine the dough ingredients in a food processor or stand mixer.) Add the lemon zest, fold in the beaten egg and liqueur, and knead briefly until the dough is smooth and pliant. Form the dough into a ball, cover with plastic wrap, and let rest in the fridge for 30 minutes.

Preheat the oven to 350°F (180°C). Grease an 8-inch (20-cm) tart pan with butter or olive oil.

On a floured surface, roll out the dough and line the tart pan, cutting and patching the dough if it tears. Prick the base all over with a fork and press the dough into the walls of the pan.

To make the filling, in a small bowl, break up the cheese with a fork into a coarse mash. In a medium bowl, beat the eggs with the granulated sugar, then add the cheese and chopped mint, mixing well.

Pour the filling into the prepared pastry shell. Bake in the oven until firm and lightly browned on top, about 35 minutes.

Transfer the pan to a wire rack and let cool. Dust with superfine sugar and decorate with the mint leaves.

WINE SUGGESTION: A FRESHLY FRUITY, SWEET MOSCATEL OR OTHER DESSERT WINE

Mel is honey, and *mató* is a fresh cheese no more than a day or two old. Pearly white, cool, and creamy, with the taste of fresh milk, it is a cheese that is only just barely a cheese. The most widely available equivalent is probably ricotta, although any fresh curd cheese will do fine.

mel i mató

1 lb (500 g) *mató* or other fresh curd cheese such as whole-milk ricotta

4–6 ripe figs, about 6 oz (170 g) total weight

½ cup (6 oz/170 g) light, aromatic honey such as orange blossom

serves 4

If using *mató,* cut the cheese into slices 1 inch (2.5 cm) thick and arrange on individual plates. Alternatively, if the cheese is not solid enough to slice, spoon it onto the plates.

Using a small, sharp knife, remove the woody stems from the figs. Cut each fig into quarters lengthwise and arrange them, flesh side up, next to the cheese on each plate.

Drizzle the honey evenly over the cheese and figs and serve at once.

WINE SUGGESTION: A GOLDEN, SILKY MOSCATEL FROM ALICANTE

These days, quince paste, or *membrillo*, is easy enough to find in specialty food markets. But it's worth making up a batch at home—it will probably be nicer than the store-bought version, and a pot of *membrillo* makes a great Christmas gift. Look out for quinces in farmers' markets in late fall.

homemade quince preserves

FOR THE QUINCE PRESERVES

2 lb (1 kg) quinces

3½–4 cups (1½–1¾ lb/ 700–800 g) sugar

1 teaspoon ground cinnamon (optional)

Fresh soft cream cheese, a youngish Manchego, or a mild goat cheese for serving

Crackers or toasted bread for serving

Fresh fruit, such as grapes or sliced apples and pears, for serving

makes about 1 qt (4 cups/ 1 l) preserves

To make the quince preserves, wipe the fuzz off the quinces and rinse well. Peel each quince, cut in half, and remove the core and seeds. Reserve the peels, cores, and seeds and place in a square of cheesecloth. Bring the corners together and tie securely with kitchen string.

Slice the quinces and place in a heavy nonreactive pot of stainless steel or enamel-lined cast iron. Add about 1 qt (4 cups/1 l) water to cover and the cheesecloth pouch. Bring to a boil, reduce the heat to low, and cook slowly, uncovered, until very tender, 20–40 minutes; the timing will vary from batch to batch. You may want to stop the cooking a few times, for about an hour or two, to let the quinces rest and redden. Add more water if the mixture begins to dry out.

When the quinces are red and very tender, remove and discard the cheesecloth bag. Drain off and reserve the cooking water. Using a potato masher, mash the quinces, or purée them in a food processor. In the same pot, combine the pulp and the reserved cooking water, 3½ cups (1½ lb/700 g) of the sugar, and the cinnamon and cook very slowly over low heat, stirring often, until thick, about 20 minutes. Taste and add more sugar if the preserves seem too tart.

Ladle into hot, sterilized canning jars to within ¼ inch (6 mm) of the top. Wipe each rim clean with a clean, hot, damp kitchen towel, cover with a sterilized canning lid, and seal tightly with a screw band. Process the jars in a hot-water bath for 10 minutes. Check the seals, label, and store in a cool pantry for up to 1 year. Jars that do not form a good seal can be refrigerated for up to 1 month.

Serve the quince preserves with a cheese (or selection of cheeses), crackers, and fruit.

COOK'S NOTE: Add a few skinned walnuts towards the end of cooking.

WINE SUGGESTION: A NEW-GENERATION SPANISH SWEET RED WINE LIKE THE CASTAÑO DULCE FROM BODEGAS CASTAÑO (D.O. YECLA)

Rincón de Pepe is Murcia's most famous restaurant, and a byword for unpretentious cooking that takes good care with the excellent local fish, vegetables, and citrus fruit. I first ate these fascinating fritters, *paparajotes*, at "Pepe's Corner," and have craved them ever since. Note that the leaves are not meant to be eaten, but serve to add a haunting lemon perfume to the crispy batter in which they're coated.

lemon-leaf fritters

16 large pesticide-free lemon leaves

2 large eggs

1 teaspoon baking powder

Pinch of fine sea salt

2 cups (500 ml) whole milk

Grated zest of 1 lemon

½ cup (3½ oz/100 g) granulated sugar

2 cups (10 oz/315 g) all-purpose flour, sifted

Olive oil for deep frying

⅓ cup (2½ oz/60 g) superfine sugar

½ teaspoon ground cinnamon

serves 4

Wash the lemon leaves and pat dry.

In a large bowl, beat the eggs with a balloon whisk until blended. Add the baking powder and salt, followed by the milk, lemon zest, and granulated sugar, mixing well. Add the flour little by little, whisking to prevent lumps, until a creamy batter forms. Place in the fridge for 30 minutes.

Pour olive oil into a wide, deep frying pan to a depth of 1 inch (2.5-cm) and heat over medium-high heat until smoking hot.

Holding each lemon leaf by the stem, coat it thinly with batter, lay it carefully in the hot oil, and fry until deep golden brown, a few seconds on each side, basting the upper side with oil before turning the leaf over.

Remove with a slotted spoon and drain on paper towels. Mix the superfine sugar with the cinnamon and dust the *paparajotes* generously with this mixture. Serve piping hot, and eat by holding a leaf by the stem and scraping the fried batter off with your teeth, like eating an artichoke leaf.

WINE SUGGESTION: A SWEET RED WINE MADE FROM THE MONASTRELL GRAPE

In recent years Spain has gone crazy for the gin and tonic, becoming the world's biggest per capita consumer of gin. Though the G&T is normally consumed as an after-lunch or nighttime tipple, this lip-smacking *sorbete* makes a brilliant opening salvo when you're hosting a crowd for a summer party.

gin & tonic sorbete

2 cups (500 ml) simple syrup (see Cook's Note)

1½ cups (350 ml) gin

2 cups (500 ml) tonic water

Juice of 2 limes, strained

1 large egg white, beaten

Zest of 2 limes, cut into thin strips

makes about 30 shot-glass servings

In a large bowl, stir together the simple syrup, gin, tonic water, and lime juice. Freeze in an ice-cream machine according to the manufacturer's instructions until almost firm, then add the egg white to the mix and continue churning until the sorbet is firm.

Serve in ice-cold shot glasses and decorate each with a thin strip of lime zest.

COOK'S NOTES: Simple syrup is a mixture of water and sugar, boiled and allowed to cool. I recommend making a larger quantity than is needed for this recipe. It keeps well in the fridge, and will come in handy for making other sorbets as well as cocktails. Heat 4 cups (1¾ lb/800 g) sugar with 4 cups (1 l) water until the sugar has dissolved. Turn off the heat and allow to cool, then place in the fridge until completely cold.

This recipe includes uncooked egg.

For the most delicate flavor and the creamiest texture, serve this stove-top rice pudding cool, not chilled. Spanish cooks regularly use cinnamon in their desserts. Here, it infuses the pudding and provides an attractive and flavorful garnish. Use a rasp grater for grating the cinnamon stick over the top of the finished pudding.

rice pudding with cinnamon

4½ cups (1.1 l) half-and-half

⅔ cup (5 oz/130 g) sugar

1 tablespoon grated lemon zest, plus more for garnish

1 tablespoon grated orange zest, plus more for garnish

2 cinnamon sticks

½ vanilla bean, split lengthwise

1 cup (7 oz/220 g) short-grain Spanish rice such as Bomba or Calasparra

serves 6–8

In a saucepan over medium-high heat, stir together the half-and-half, 1½ cups (350 ml) water, the sugar, lemon and orange zests, and 1 of the cinnamon sticks. Using the tip of a small knife, scrape the seeds from the vanilla bean into the mixture and then add the pod. Stir in the rice. Place over medium-high heat and bring the mixture to just below a boil.

Reduce the heat to maintain a brisk simmer and cook uncovered, stirring often, until the rice is tender but some liquid remains, 35–45 minutes. The pudding should have the consistency of thin oatmeal.

Remove and discard the cinnamon stick and vanilla bean. Spoon the pudding into individual dessert bowls or into a 2-qt (2-l) terra-cotta casserole. Let cool to room temperature, then cover and refrigerate until cool, at least 1 hour or up to 1 day. Grate lemon and orange zest and cinnamon from the other stick over the top just before serving.

WINE SUGGESTION: A COLD GLASS OF SWEET, AGED SHERRY FROM THE PEDRO XIMÉNEZ GRAPE

basic recipes

FISH STOCK

2½ lb (1.25 kg) fish bones, heads, and skin (see Cook's Note), well rinsed

1 large yellow onion, coarsely chopped

½ fennel bulb, trimmed and coarsely chopped

3 ribs celery, coarsely chopped

1 carrot, peeled and diced

1 leek, white and pale green parts, chopped

2 cups (500 ml) dry white wine

Kosher or sea salt

MAKES ABOUT 2 QT (2 L)

In a large saucepan, combine the fish parts, onion, fennel, celery, carrot, leek, 6 cups (1.5 l) water, and wine. Bring to a boil over medium heat, skimming off any foamy impurities from the surface. Cover partially, reduce the heat to low, and simmer until the fish flesh starts to fall off the bones, about 25 minutes.

Line a colander with damp cheesecloth and place over a clean container. Strain the stock through the colander. Season to taste with salt. Use at once or let cool, cover tightly, and refrigerate the stock for up to 3 days or freeze for up to 3 months.

COOK'S NOTE: Ask your fishmonger to set aside some fish bones, sometimes called frames, or parts for you. Bones or parts from lean fish, such as cod, red snapper, flounder, and sole, are ideal. Avoid using bones from oily fish. Be sure the gills have been removed and the skin, if any, is free of scales.

CHICKEN STOCK

1 chicken, 4–5 lb (1.8–2.2 kg)

2 whole cloves

2 yellow onions, quartered

3 carrots, cut into 2-inch (5-cm) pieces

2 ribs celery, including leafy tops, cut into 2-inch (5-cm) pieces

1 cup (1½ oz/45 g) chopped fresh flat-leaf parsley

4 fresh thyme sprigs (optional)

½ teaspoon peppercorns

Kosher or sea salt

MAKES 2–2½ QT (2–2.5 L)

Put the chicken in a large stockpot. Stick the cloves into 2 onion quarters and add them to the pot with the remaining onion quarters, carrots, celery, parsley, thyme (if using), and peppercorns. Add water to cover by about 2 inches (5 cm) and bring to a boil over medium-high heat, skimming off any foamy impurities from the surface. Reduce the heat to low and simmer gently, uncovered, skimming any foam as it appears, until reduced by about half, 3–4 hours. Season to taste with salt during the last hour of cooking.

Lift out the chicken from the pot, remove the skin and bones, and reserve the meat for use in soups. Line a colander with damp cheesecloth and place over a clean container. Strain the stock through the colander. Let cool to room temperature, then cover and refrigerate until well chilled. Skim off and discard the congealed layer of fat on the surface before using. If not using at once, refrigerate the stock for up to 5 days or freeze for up to 3 months.

VEGETABLE STOCK

10 cups (2½ lb/1.25 kg) cut-up assorted vegetables such as leeks, celery, tomatoes, mushrooms, green beans, spinach, and Swiss chard

1 yellow onion, coarsely chopped

1 carrot, coarsely chopped

12 sprigs fresh flat-leaf parsley

Leaves from 4 sprigs fresh thyme

1 bay leaf

MAKES 2–3 QT (2–3 L)

Put the assorted vegetables, onion, and carrot in a stockpot. Place the parsley, thyme, and bay leaf on a square of cheesecloth, bring the corners together, tie securely with kitchen string, and add to the pot. Add cold water to cover by 3 inches (7.5 cm), bring to a boil, and then immediately reduce the heat to low. Simmer, uncovered, until the stock is aromatic and flavorful, 1–1½ hours, adding water as needed to maintain the original level. Remove from the heat and pour the stock through a fine-mesh sieve into a clean container. Use at once, or let cool to room temperature, then cover and refrigerate for up to 1 week or freeze for up to 3 months.

BEEF STOCK

6 lb (3 kg) meaty beef and veal shanks

2 yellow onions, coarsely chopped

1 leek, including about 6 inches (15 cm) of the green tops, coarsely chopped

2 carrots, coarsely chopped

1 rib celery, coarsely chopped

6 cloves garlic

4 sprigs fresh flat-leaf parsley

3 sprigs fresh thyme

2 small bay leaves

10 peppercorns

Kosher or sea salt

MAKES 4–5 QT (4–5 L)

In a stockpot, combine the beef and veal shanks and add cold water to cover. Place the pot over medium-high heat and slowly bring almost to a boil, skimming off any foamy impurities from the surface. Reduce the heat to low and simmer uncovered for 2 hours, skimming the surface as needed and adding more water if necessary to keep the shanks immersed.

Add the onions, leek, carrots, celery, garlic, parsley, thyme, bay leaves, and peppercorns and continue to simmer over low heat, uncovered and skimming any foam as it appears, until the meat begins to fall from the bones and the stock is very flavorful, about 2 hours longer. Season to taste with salt during the last hour of cooking.

Remove from the heat and let stand until the liquid is almost room temperature, about 1 hour. Using a slotted spoon, lift out the meat and reserve for another use. Place a colander over a clean large vessel. Strain the stock through the colander, then line the colander with damp cheesecloth and strain again. Pour the stock into 1 or 2 containers (with lids) and let the stock cool to room temperature, then cover and refrigerate until well chilled. Skim off and discard the congealed layer of fat on the surface before using. If not using immediately, refrigerate the stock for up to 5 days or freeze for up to 3 months.

HAM STOCK

1 piece of ham bone (see Cook's Note)

2 carrots, trimmed

1 yellow onion, peeled

1 leek, white and pale green parts, trimmed

2 sprigs fresh flat-leaf parsley

2 tablespoons olive oil

MAKES ABOUT 2½ QT (2.5 L)

In a stockpot or large saucepan, combine the ham bone, carrots, onion, leek, and parsley. Fill the pot with cold water and bring to a boil, skimming off any foamy impurities from the surface.

Reduce the heat to low. Add the olive oil and simmer gently until the liquid has reduced by half, 2–3 hours.

Line a colander with damp cheesecloth and place over a clean container. Strain the broth through the colander. Let cool to room temperature, then cover and refrigerate until well chilled. Skim off and discard the congealed layer of fat on the surface before using. If not using immediately, refrigerate the stock for up to 5 days or freeze for up to 3 months.

COOK'S NOTE: Spanish cooks often use a piece of bone left over when all the meat has been cut away from a serrano ham. The bone should be divided into fist-sized pieces with a handsaw (ask your butcher to do this for you). Alternatively, vacuum-packed ham bone pieces can be found at specialty grocers.

TOMATE FRITO

½ cup (125 ml) olive oil

1 large yellow onion, chopped

2 cloves garlic, minced

2 lb (1 kg) ripe tomatoes, peeled, cored, and roughly chopped (see Cook's Note)

Fine sea salt

MAKES ABOUT 3 CUPS (750 ML)

In a large saucepan, heat the olive oil over medium heat and sauté the onion until tender and lightly browned, about 12 minutes. Stir in the garlic and sauté for 1 minute more.

Add the chopped tomato and 1 tablespoon salt. Reduce the heat to medium-low and gently cook, stirring with a wooden spoon, until the tomato has almost disintegrated and has taken on a rich, dark color, about 20 minutes.

Allow to cool a little, then transfer to a kitchen blender. Liquidize to a smooth purée.

COOK'S NOTE: If you can't find really ripe and tasty tomatoes, canned tomatoes offer good results. Drain them before adding to the pan.

ALLIOLI

4 cloves garlic

3 tablespoons fresh lemon juice

Coarse sea salt

2 cups (500 ml) extra-virgin olive oil (see Cook's Note)

MAKES SLIGHTLY MORE THAN 2 CUPS (500 ML)

To make the *allioli,* in a mortar and pestle, combine the garlic cloves, lemon juice, and ½ teaspoon salt and pound to a smooth paste. Add the olive oil, first in single drops, mixing between each drop, then in small drips, then in a thin stream. Do not hurry the process, or the mixture will curdle. Use the pestle to crush and stir, working always in the same direction. You should end up with a greenish, jellylike emulsion.

COOK'S NOTE: Extra-virgin olive oil produces an intensely flavored, dark-colored *allioli.* If you prefer a lighter taste, use a mixture of olive oil with sunflower or peanut oil, or choose a lower-grade olive oil.

FLATBREAD DOUGH

1⅔ cups (8 oz/250 g) unbleached all-purpose flour

2 teaspoons baking powder

Fine sea salt

1 tablespoon olive oil, plus more for greasing

1 large egg yolk

MAKES ENOUGH DOUGH FOR 1 FLATBREAD (PAGE 38)

Sift the flour, baking powder, and ½ teaspoon salt into a bowl. Make a well in the flour and add the olive oil and egg yolk. Gradually add ¾ cup (180 ml) water, mixing the wet ingredients into the flour little by little with a wooden spoon.

On a lightly floured board, knead the dough until soft, smooth, and elastic, about 1 minute. Form the dough into a ball and place in a large, lightly oiled bowl. Cover with a kitchen towel and let stand in a warm place until the dough puffs slightly, about 30 minutes. Use as directed in a recipe.

ROASTING BELL PEPPERS

Preheat the broiler and set a rack about 6 inches (15 cm) from the heat source. Place a bell pepper on a baking sheet and broil, turning occasionally with tongs, until the skin is blistered and charred black on all sides, about 15 minutes.

Place the pepper in a bowl and cover. Let stand until cool enough to handle. Peel away the blackened skin and remove and discard the stem. Slit the pepper open, then remove and discard the seeds and ribs. Scrape away any remaining blackened skin with a small knife.

TOASTING NUTS

Set a rack in the middle of the oven and preheat to 325°F (165°C). Spread the almonds in a single layer in a pie pan. Toast, stirring occasionally, until the nuts are fragrant and their color deepens, about 5 minutes. Remove from the oven and let cool.

PEELING & SEEDING TOMATOES

Cut a shallow X in the blossom end of each tomato. Immerse in a pan of boiling water until the peel begins to peel away from the X, about 30 seconds. Transfer to a bowl of ice water to cool, then peel away the skin. To seed, cut in half crosswise and squeeze each half gently to dislodge the seeds, scooping them out with your fingers.

drinks

SPANISH HOT CHOCOLATE

4 cups (1 l) whole milk

½ teaspoon saffron threads, lightly crushed

1 or 2 cinnamon sticks

1 whole dried árbol chile or pequin chile

½ vanilla bean, split lengthwise

¼ cup (2 oz/50 g) sugar

4 oz (125 g) bittersweet chocolate, coarsely chopped

SERVES 4

Combine the milk, saffron threads, cinnamon stick(s), chile, vanilla bean, and sugar in a large, heavy saucepan. Bring just to a boil over medium heat, stirring to dissolve the sugar, then reduce the heat to medium-low and simmer for 10 minutes. Remove from the heat and let steep for 10 minutes. Strain into a large pot, discarding the solids. Heat again gently, then add the bittersweet chocolate. Whisk briskly for 5 minutes to dissolve the chocolate and make a frothy head. Serve at once.

SANGRÍA

6 ice cubes

1 bottle (750 ml) fruity dry red wine

¼ cup (60 ml) Spanish brandy

2 tablespoons sugar

1–2 lemons, sliced paper-thin

2 Valencia oranges, sliced paper-thin and then quartered

3 cups (750 ml) sparkling water

SERVES 4

Put the ice cubes in a pitcher. Pour in the bottle of wine, then add the brandy, sugar, fruit slices, and sparkling water. Stir well, pour into chilled glasses, and sip slowly to beat the heat of an Andalucían afternoon.

HORCHATA

1 cup (5 oz/155 g) tiger nuts, soaked for 24 hours at room temperature in water to cover by 2 inches (5 cm)

4 cups (1 l) hot water

¼ cup plus 1 tablespoon (2 oz/60 g) sugar

¼ teaspoon kosher salt

Ice cubes for serving

Ground cinnamon for serving

SERVES 4

Line a colander with a double layer of cheesecloth and set it over a deep bowl. Drain the soaked tiger nuts and put them in a blender. Add the hot water and blitz on high speed until well blended and almost smooth, about 2 minutes. Carefully strain through the cheesecloth-lined colander. Gather the ends of the cheesecloth together and squeeze out the remaining liquid. Discard solids.

Add the sugar and salt to the *horchata* and whisk to combine. Let cool completely, then transfer to a clean container (with a lid) and store in the refrigerator for up to 1 week. Serve the *horchata* over ice, sprinkled with cinnamon.

COOK'S NOTE: While Mexican-style *horchata* is made from rice milk and almonds, in Valencia, *horchata* is made from ground *chufas,* or tiger nuts. These are actually little tubers, with an appealing coconut flavor. Now, thanks to the Internet, tiger nuts can be found outside of Spain.

spanish pantry staples

ALMONDS Spaniards take their almonds seriously: the Marcona variety has gained a worldwide reputation for its extreme snackability. Many recipes in this book call either for blanched, or peeled, almonds, or for flaked, or sliced, almonds.

ANCHOVIES Whether white *(boquerones),* cured, or smoked, anchovies are a common ingredient in the Spanish pantry. Cured anchovy fillets, packed in olive oil or salt, are commonly eaten as a snack on toast or as an ingredient in myriad dishes. Look for imported Spanish ones for the most delicate flavor and appealing smooth texture.

BEANS Humble beans, economical and high in protein, have always played a key role in the Spanish diet. Look for dried beans in markets with a high turnover to ensure they have not been sitting on the shelf for too long—the older the bean, the longer it will take to cook. Good-quality canned beans are a convenient choice; rinse well and drain before using. Fresh beans will taste best in their natural season.

Fava From springtime into summer, gardens throughout Spain yield profuse crops of fava beans. As the long, wide pods grow older, the inner skin on each bean thickens. Select small pods for the tenderest fava beans, and blanch older beans to help remove their tough inner skins.

Romano Also called Italian beans, these edible-pod beans have broader, flatter pods and a more robust flavor and texture than the more common green bean.

BREAD CRUMBS Fresh or dried, these are the good cook's secret weapon, bestowing a crisp topping on casseroles and a crunchy coating on panfried and roasted meats. Fresh bread crumbs are best made from slightly stale bread. French breads and baguettes, coarse country-style white breads, whole-wheat breads, and egg breads all make good fresh crumbs. Fresh crumbs will keep in a zippered plastic bag in the refrigerator for up to 1 month. Dried bread crumbs, made by toasting fresh crumbs (or purchasing them ready-made) deliver an especially light, crisp texture.

CASSOLA The thick walls of this round, shallow earthenware pan, also known as a *cazuela,* allow foods to cook gently and evenly. Ideal for long, slow cooking in the oven, the orange terra-cotta of a *cassola* is traditionally glazed only on the inside surface. Season a new *cassola* by immersing it in water for 6 hours. Repeat this soaking occasionally if you live in a dry climate or if you plan to use the pan over the direct flame of a stove top. To prevent cracks, do not heat the pan while it is empty, limit the temperature to very low on the stove top, and avoid temperature extremes.

CHEESE Cheeses are sometimes served as a dessert course in Spain, but they are more commonly bar offerings, presented in cubes or wedges. Many different types are produced throughout Spain.

Cabrales Spain's signature blue-veined cheese, this specialty of Cantabria is made from a mixture of sheep's, goat's, and cow's milk, formed into short cylinders, and aged in limestone caves for 3–6 months. It is comparable in flavor to French Roquefort, but somewhat sharper in flavor.

Idiazábal This Basque sheep's milk cheese is smoky and sharp.

Mahón The dairy cow was brought to Mallorca by the British in the eighteenth century, so it's not surprising that the island's signature cheese, Mahón, resembles England's famed cow's milk Cheddar. Mahón comes in *semi-sec* (semi-dry) and *sec* (dry) styles, its flavor and texture changing depending on the length of time it is aged.

Manchego Spain's most famous cheese, this specialty of the La Mancha region is traditionally made from sheep's milk, although cow's milk is sometimes used as well nowadays. It has a rich, tangy flavor and a firm, somewhat brittle texture.

Queso Fresco de Burgos This fresh sheep's milk cheese is produced in Castile and León, a province in the north of Spain. Made in 2- to 6-pound (1- to 3-kg) cylinders and often including some cow's milk, this very fresh, rindless cheese, mild in flavor and white in color, is very popular served with fruit for breakfast all across Spain.

Torta del Casar An Extremaduran speciality, *torta* is made from raw sheep's milk cheese and has the unusual distinction of being renneted with cardoon, a wild thistle related to the artichoke, which results in a slightly bitter, herbaceous flavor and a soft, runny interior texture.

CHESTNUTS These treasured nuts are grown in the regions surrounding the Pyrenees, where during the autumn months you can purchase the fresh, hot, starchy-sweet delicacies from street vendors. Cooked and canned chestnuts are available, but fresh ones are worth the extra bit of work needed to remove the tough mahogany-colored shells.

CHICKPEAS Also known as garbanzo or ceci beans, these nutrient-rich legumes are a staple in many Mediterranean cuisines. The round, beige beans are rich and nutty in flavor, and their firm texture holds up well to long cooking. Rinse and drain canned chickpeas well before using.

CHORIZO There are countless variations on this distinctive Iberian sausage. Made of air-dried pork and heavily spiced with garlic and paprika, chorizo sausage has a rich, smoky-sweet flavor with a hint of tanginess. Each region has its own special style, which may be mild or spicy, fresh or cured, air-dried or wood-smoked. There are two basic categories of chorizo: sausages meant for cooking, and those cured for eating uncooked, although some versions can be eaten both hot and cold. In the kitchen, chorizo is most often used in small amounts as a flavoring, adding depth to stocks, sauces, fillings, tortillas, eggs, and bean dishes. Versions from Spain tend not to be as spicy-hot as Mexican-style chorizo, but the latter may be used as a substitute.

FIDEO Called *fideu* in Catalunya, the only region in Spain where pasta is widely used, these very thin, vermicelli-like noodles appear in a local version of paella. *Fideos* are also used in a variety of soups, stews, and vegetable dishes. Look for small bags of the pasta in Spanish or Latin American markets, or use the thinnest possible angel hair pasta you can find, broken in half or into short lengths.

MORTAR & PESTLE Many aromatic ingredients, such as garlic, release more of their oils when crushed and ground in a mortar and pestle than when cut in a food processor or blender. Look for a generously sized marble or stone bowl when selecting a mortar, to allow easier and more efficient crushing. A proper *allioli* or romesco sauce, some Catalans would insist, is best served right in the rough-hewn mortar in which it was made.

NYORA PEPPERS Also spelled "*ñora*," these peppers are essential for an authentic romesco sauce. Grown mainly in Catalunya, plum-sized *nyora* peppers lend their red color, sweet flavor, and mildly spicy heat to numerous local dishes. To prepare the dried peppers, cover with boiling water and soak for 10 minutes, then scrape the flesh from inside the skins. Dried ancho chiles can be substituted.

OILS Flavor and smoke point are the two primary considerations when choosing an oil. Oils with a high smoke point are ideal for sautéing and frying. Highly flavorful oils, such as extra-virgin olive oil and toasted hazelnut oil, have a low smoke point and are best kept for drizzling on finished dishes.

Olive oil Spain and other countries in the Mediterranean region produce excellent olive oils. Processing young olives yields green oils; mature olives produce a buttery, golden oil. The highest grade is labeled "extra-virgin," which refers to cold pressing the fruit without the use of heat or chemicals. At their best, extra-virgin olive oils are clear and greenish, and taste fruity and sometimes slightly peppery. Save your best oils for finishing dishes, as heat will destroy their character.

OLIVES The bitter fruit of a hardy tree, olives must be cured before they can be eaten. Brine-cured olives stay plump, smooth, and relatively firm. Salt- or oil-cured olives become dry, wrinkled, and pleasantly bitter. Color depends on where the fruit was harvested.

Arbequina Most Arbequina table olives are grown in eastern Spain, Aragon and Catalunya, near the French border. Arbequinas have a firm texture, with a color ranging from pale green to medium brown and a sweet flavor that falls in between that of a green and a black olive.

Manzanilla These are the classic green Spanish olives: a large, meaty fruit, with purple-tinged green skin and a rich, salty flavor. Manzanillas—which means "little apples"—originated near Seville.

PAELLA PAN Spain's famous rice dish is traditionally cooked outdoors in a wide, shallow metal pan placed over a fast-burning wood fire. Made of rolled steel and sporting two round handles, a paella pan can measure from 10 inches (25 cm) to more than 3 feet (1 m) across. A 12- or 14-inch (30- or 35-cm) pan easily fits 3 to 4 generous servings. Paella pans should be seasoned and cleaned like woks and cast-iron pans: avoid using soap when washing, dry thoroughly, and then coat with a thin film of oil before using.

PICADA A Catalan sauce based on ground nuts, typically almonds or hazelnuts, thickened with toasted bread and flavored with garlic, saffron, paprika, parsley, vinegar, or wine, a *picada* gives rich body and depth of flavor when stirred into a stew. Some, like Mexico's mole sauces, include bittersweet chocolate.

PIMENTÓN A spice made from dried smoked red peppers, Spanish *pimentón* is available in sweet *(dulce)*, bittersweet *(agridulce)*, and spicy *(picante)* forms. True *pimentón* is increasingly findable in specialty food stores in the United States, packed in small charming tins. Cookbooks will often say to use paprika in its place, but this makes a poor substitute.

RICE Brought to Spain by the Moors, rice became an important crop in the marshlands of southern Spain, where shorter-grain japonica varieties thrive. Calasparra and Valencia rice, medium-short-grain varieties, and short Bomba rice are still considered the best for paella. Connoisseurs of Spanish rice refer to its *perla*, the pearl of starch at each grain's core that soaks up the flavors of other ingredients. Italian Arborio or Carnaroli rice is the closest equivalent, but requires a different quantity of liquid to cook properly.

SAFFRON Known as *azafrán* in Spain, this spice takes its name from the Arabic word for "yellow," evoking the bright hue it lends to dishes. Saffron threads, the dried stigmas of a purple crocus flower, are still gathered by hand, one reason the spice is comparatively rare and costly. Introduced to Iberia by the Moors, it has become a signature seasoning in Spanish dishes, particularly paella.

SERRANO HAM The rich, sweet-salty punch of flavorful serrano, made from the white *landrace* breed of pig, makes it a natural partner for dry sherry. *Jamón serrano* is the general term for cured ham, similar to Italy's prosciutto. The hams are cured with salt for as long as 2 weeks, and then hung to mature, sometimes for up to 2 years. Serrano is the Spanish ham best known outside Spain, but it's not the only one (or, frankly, the best): excellent *jamon ibérico* is produced from the black Iberian pig, raised in forests in Extremadura, western Andalucía, and western New Castile, where it dines on grasses, acorns, and olives. Some of these hams are aged as long as 36 months.

SHERRY Sherry takes its name from its place of origin, Jerez, a region of southwest Spain where Phoenician settlers first introduced wine grapes. Blended and fortified, sherry wines fall into several styles. Dry or very dry fino has a straw color and a delicate flavor that makes it ideal for tapas. Manzanilla, a lighter, bitter wine, is fino produced in the seaside town of Sanúcar de Barrameda. It pairs with

shellfish particularly well. Amber-hued Amontadillo is a medium-dry wine with a rich, nutty flavor that complements smoked meats and cheese. Medium-sweet oloroso develops a dark mahogany color and walnut flavor; serve it with sausage, nuts, or dried fruits. Sweet cream sherry is a dessert wine.

SOFREGIT Many Catalan recipes start with this basic preparation. Although Catalan cooks add ingredients like tomatoes, bell peppers, garlic, carrots, or *pimentón* the essential combination remains that of onions and olive oil. *Sofregit* adds a distinctive sweet-savory flavor to Catalan cuisine. Other regions of Spain refer to it as *sofrito*.

TOMATOES Tomatoes were first cultivated in Spain during the early sixteenth century. In Spanish kitchens, the narrow, firm Roma, or plum, tomato predominates, for its deep flavor and ability to hold up to long cooking.

VINEGARS The term *vinegar* refers to any alcoholic liquid caused to ferment a second time by certain strains of yeast, turning it highly acidic. Vinegars highlight the qualities of the liquid from which they are made. Red wine vinegar, for example, has a more robust flavor than vinegar produced from white wine. Sherry vinegar is indispensable to the Spanish pantry.

index

weldon**owen**

Weldon Owen is a division of Bonnier Publishing
1045 Sansome Street, Suite 100, San Francisco, CA 94111
www.weldonowen.com

WELDON OWEN, INC.

President & Publisher Roger Shaw
SVP, Sales & Marketing Amy Kaneko
Finance & Operations Director Philip Paulick

Associate Publisher Amy Marr
Project Editor Sarah Putman Clegg
Associate Editor Emma Rudolph

Creative Director Kelly Booth
Art Director Marisa Kwek
Senior Production Designer Rachel Lopez Metzger

Production Director Chris Hemesath
Associate Production Director Michelle Duggan

Imaging Manager Don Hill

Photographer Maren Caruso
Food Stylist Robyn Valarik
Prop Stylist Laura Cook

Rustic Spanish

Conceived and produced by Weldon Owen, Inc.
In collaboration with Williams-Sonoma, Inc.
3250 Van Ness Avenue, San Francisco, CA 94109

A WELDON OWEN PRODUCTION
Copyright © 2016 Weldon Owen, Inc.
and Williams-Sonoma, Inc.

Library of Congress Cataloging-in-Publication
data is available.

ISBN 13: 978-1-68188-103-4
ISBN 10: 1-68188-103-9

Printed and bound in China by 1010 Printing, Ltd.

First printed in 2016
10 9 8 7 6 5 4 3 2

ACKNOWLEDGMENTS

Weldon Owen wishes to thank the following people for their generous support
in producing this book: Kris Balloun, Pranavi Chopra, Sean Franzen,
Gloria Geller, Erin O'Connell, Elizabeth Parson, and Nicole Twohy.